Advance praise for

His Hands, His Tools, His Sex, His Dress: Lesbian Writers on Their Fathers

"This anthology is a stunner–one of the best collections I have ever come across. The writing is first-rate and the topic–lesbians' positive recollections of their fathers–is a subject that has never before been mined. The dudes and the dorks, the pranksters and the philanderers, the romantics and the rogues that pour out of these pages are irresistible. Radical dyke feminist separatist that I am, I loved 'em all. Goddess forgive me."

–Marny Hall, psychotherapist and
author of *The Lavender Couch* and *The Lesbian Love Companion*

"At last, a book about the father-daughter lesbian relationship–the identifications, attractions, conflicts, and joys. A must read."

–Suzanne Iasenza, psychologist/ sex therapist and co-editor
of *Lesbians and Psychoanalysis*

D1563464

His Hands, His Tools, His Sex, His Dress:

Lesbian Writers on Their Fathers

Alice Street Editions
Judith P. Stelboum
Editor-in-Chief

Past Perfect, by Judith P. Stelboum

Inside Out, by Juliet Carrera

Façades, by Alex Marcoux

Weeding at Dawn: A Lesbian Country Life, by Hawk Madrone

His Hands, His Tools, His Sex, His Dress: Lesbian Writers on Their Fathers, edited by Catherine Reid and Holly K. Iglesias

Forthcoming

Yin Fire, by Alexandra Grilikhes

Treat, by Angie Vicars

From Flitch to Ash: A Musing on Trees and Carving by Diane Derrick

Egret, by Helen Collins

Extraordinary Couples, Ordinary Lives, by Lynn Haley-Banez and Joanne Garrett

Foreword

Alice Street Editions provides a voice for established as well up-coming lesbian writers, reflecting the diversity of lesbian interests, ethnicities, ages and class. This cutting edge series of novels, memoirs, and non-fiction writing welcomes the opportunity to present controversial views, explore multicultural ideas, encourage debate, and inspire creativity from a variety of lesbian perspectives. Through enlightening, illuminating and provocative writing, Alice Street Editions can make a significant contribution to the visibility and accessibility of lesbian writing, and bring lesbian/focused writing to a wider audience. Recognizing our own desires and ideas in print is life sustaining, acknowledging the reality of who we are, our place in the world, individually and collectively.

Judith P. Stelboum
Editor-in-Chief
Alice Street Editions

His Hands, His Tools, His Sex, His Dress:
Lesbian Writers on Their Fathers

Catherine Reid
Holly K. Iglesias
Editors

Alice Street Editions
Harrington Park Press
New York • London • Oxford

Published by

Alice Street Editions, Harrington Park Press®, an imprint of The Haworth Press, Inc., 10 Alice Street, Binghamton, NY 13904-1580 USA (www.HaworthPress.com).

Cover design by Thomas J. Mayshock Jr.

Library of Congress Cataloging-in-Publication Data

His hands, his tools, his sex, his dress : lesbian writers on their fathers / Catherine Reid, Holly K. Iglesias, editors.
    p. cm.
    ISBN 1-56023-210-2 (alk. paper)–ISBN 1-56023-211-0 (pbk. : alk. paper)
    1. Fathers and daughters–Fiction. 2. Lesbians–Family relationships–Fiction. 3. Fathers and daughters–United States. 4. Lesbians–United States–Biography. 5. Fathers–United States–Biography. 6. Lesbians–Family relationships. 7. Lesbians' writings, American. 8. Lesbians–Fiction. 9. Fathers–Fiction. I. Reid, Catherine, 1955- II. Iglesias, Holly.
PS648.F36 H57 2000
813′2.1083520431–dc21
                                                                            00-48542

CONTENTS

His Hands, His Tools, His Sex, His Dress:

Lesbian Writers on Their Fathers

Introduction

On a cold night, I walk through the field toward our house, the brighter stars and a half moon visible in a chunk of sky between pines. The house is lit from within, the rooms clearer in detail than the constellations above me. I can see my lover, reading on the couch, and I imagine the dinner we'll soon make, the evening we'll spend together. We've only been here a few months, the house over a hundred years old, the foundation full of holes, rot in the threshold, mice in the walls, and I feel full of love for the challenge of the house, the land, the snow that will soon close us in, the skills I'll need to help make this a safe home.

In this night of air cold enough to hurry my walk, I look toward the house and feel *fatherly*. I take it on like a thick coat, readying myself to deal with beams and leaks and loose wiring, with crumbling plaster and shimmed floors and old plumbing. *Protect us and keep us.* It's a heady feeling, with lots of power attached–electric saws and sudden noise, messes of sheetrock, sawdust and paint. And it's one that comes at quiet times, too, in the fast race up the stairs, when the two-year-old niece, who's visiting for a week, shrieks awake with the wail of the three a.m. train. She's in the middle of her room when I find her, blanket in one hand, her pajamas askew. I wrap her in my arms and carry her back to sleep. *With the strength of a dad,* I think, as we curl together in her narrow bed until her breathing deepens and her body relaxes, my arms around her like an arch or a trellis, agile and strong and able to yield, too.

My father, on the other hand, rarely did manual work; he was a sixty-hour-a-week businessman, providing well for the increasing number of dependents who surrounded him. Yet despite this strict sense of duty, he had a rebellious streak, too, something I loved in

1

this taciturn Yankee, and I took secret pleasure in knowing that sometimes he couldn't be found, the few times I went by myself to the store and no one knew his whereabouts. He was his own boss, with a fierce independence, and I wanted to be just like him.

My three brothers and I, though not our other two sisters, have all learned to do what we can with our hands. One's a landscape gardener; one invents and repairs almost anything metal; the third can build a guitar, mold a kayak, tile a room. All three are abundantly generous, love good beer, and have made it a practice to learn how things work. And all three carry a resentment, right there below the surface, at having an absent father through most of their childhoods. With a focus on my mother, I cared somewhat less; instead, I took on the role that we all wished he were around to fulfill. After all, someone had to help protect the little kids; someone had to look out for the vulnerable parent whom we did count on. And I was bumped into the place of oldest-at-home, my older brother sent to a boarding school, his anger too much to contain in a house full of smaller, easily wounded bodies. And I'm tall, like my father, and I have the same boyish looks that gay friends like and have complimented in my dad.

And how it makes me shudder to think of him as a sexual being, choked and awkward should a gay man start to flirt with him. Yet it's equally odd to ponder the fact that several of my former lovers (all women) have taken up with men since parting ways with me. It makes me wonder about the appeal of this butch-femme mix to women who are more straight than queer, who yearn to find someone both rough and tender, hard and soft, able and strong and compassionate. And then I wonder how much else of my dad I'm embodying, particularly in those moments when I'm not feeling fatherly, and I leave the subject before I begin fingering my chin, searching for hairs that might start coming in.

"Most lesbians I know really like their father," writes Peggy Shaw, "me included." It's my experience, too, though I feel I hardly knew him when I was a kid, other than his love of model trains and classic cars, his habit of falling asleep when reading us bedtime stories, his hate of rice and camping, as a result of WWII–all details given extra weight because we knew so little in contrast to the hours spent with our mother. Then, too, I lost additional time in the two years we didn't speak to each other, when the political beliefs helping shape me had him leaving whatever room I happened to enter, and my trips home became even rarer. But we have each lived long enough to leave behind our more rigid positions, to find out what we like about each other, to take comfort in having time together. And from this newer, easy place, I can see our similarities; I can admit to a gratitude for the ways he sought to take care of us; I can acknowledge how I look to him for my heritage, for influencing my path.

Even though I am closer, emotionally, to my mother's side of the family; even though her roots run as deep if not deeper into the New England landscape, it's his name and his ancestors that I link myself to, a curious patrilineal focus, as though I wasn't listening all those years to the waves of feminist theorists pointing out the dangers in allying with the fathers–In the Name of the Father, Our God the Father, The Fatherland, The Father Right, Father Knows Best–as though I haven't benefited from the myriad joys and passions of my matrilineage. But there it is: my keen desire to identify with the Scot who found his way to Nova Scotia and then down to Vermont, the Reid whose traits passed directly to my father–self-effacing, hard-working, morally correct, forbearing– and then to me (though diluted), along with a skin prone to cancer, a spine known for rigidity, and blue eyes that call people in.

And I want to be for my lover much of who he is to my mother, clear-thinking and sturdy and practical. I want to convey trust, one of the greatest gifts I have received from him, when he hands over the keys to his car, his truck, his house, his money, his belief in me enhancing every decision I make. And I want to be tender, for years the emotion he rarely let anyone see, and that erupts from him now in such sudden moments that I feel unshielded and fearless when tears pool in his eyes and he doesn't turn away.

I also want plenty of times when I am nothing like him, when no one confuses us, when no one thinks to ask if I'm his daughter. He's sober and deliberate, an only child who was delicate, who spent too much time playing alone, and somehow grew up to sire a brood the size of which still startles him. I imagine sex to be the one impulse he allowed himself, and moderation be damned (the two of them finding each other late at night, his surprise at his appetite, her Yes, his fast need). He's defenseless against our teasings; at a loss for what to do with our wrestlings, our noise, our bawdy, bodily mess. And me: I don't want to be confined to the dark, to be muffled by bedclothes. I need to be rash and immoderate, passionate and unencumbered, full of the boy-energy my brothers wanted and bucked against, the kind that makes them squirm if they indulge in it too long.

And as a consequence of being his daughter, I get to straddle gender lines, playing his part to my mother, embodying her in my more intimate moments. And though I didn't lose my mother, as did Laura Markowitz, my desires echo hers in the kind of protection I wanted and emulated: "I want to be a woman like my mother: outspoken, joyful, ready to laugh. I want to be a man like my father: gentle, generous, in control. . . . I thought if I was just like him, I would never feel sadness, anger, fear. I wanted to wear my skin the way he wore his, wrapped in a wall of muscle through which nothing could hurt. I thought I could escape the fate of my mother, who was sickly, who was weak, who died. I relied on him to be infallible."

In the first anthology Holly and I edited, *Every Woman I've Ever Loved: Lesbian Writers on Their Mothers,* we found images full of yearning and fury, passion and ire, for the mother the daughters did or did not have, for the traces or absence of her in other women lovers. Tackling the topic of mother meant tapping a rich, deep fuel; the fine crafting of each work barely contains the raw power pulsing within.

When we began asking writers to reveal their fathers to us, we were surprised by the discomfort or resistance we encountered ("I can't do it now! Ask me in twenty years!"), suggesting more emotional charge than is typically associated with this cooler, more detached parent. And certainly more than is found in lesbian novels, where fathers tend to be killed off early (*Revolution of Little Girls*; *Bastard Out of Carolina*; the rock-and-roll dad in *Cavedweller*); appear absent or ineffective (*Ghost Dance*; *Red Azalea*; Judith Katz's fictional fathers); or are benign as household furniture (*Rubyfruit Jungle*; *Oranges Are Not the Only Fruit*). Shay Youngblood's novel *Soul Kiss* explores the new territory of sexual tension between a daughter and father, who find in each other something they both want from the absent mother, but the girl flees before it consummates and the story ends with her still in adolescence. We're left to speculate on any lasting effect of the artist-father on her life.

The persistent cultural stereotype of dykes and dads further complicates this query of who the father really is. In this caricature, his cruelty traumatizes his daughter right into the arms of a woman, the only sex with whom she will ever feel safe. What we have found again and again, however, in our own experiences and in the writings for this collection, is an expansiveness towards fathers as a result of being lesbian: Not only can we love what is best about our dads (without having to unravel the dislikes in intimate relationships with men), but, by choosing a partner of the same sex, we can simultaneously celebrate what we love about women.

And here is where I disagree with the theory of a psychoanalyst friend, a straight woman who believes that though feminism gave women permission to be angry at men, women have failed feminism in being consistently more grateful than angry at their fathers. She cites as evidence some of the books that have appeared in the past few years by such noted straight authors as

Germaine Greer, Mona Simpson, and Mary Gordon (*Daddy, We Hardly Knew You; The Lost Father;* and *The Shadow Man,* respectively). Each deals with a prolonged search for the man who abandoned his daughter or fabricated his existence, but rage at the father plays little part in any of these quests; he remains elusive, delusive, easy to mythologize, easy to adore.

I counter her claim with the evidence of this anthology, which suggests that lesbians may, in fact, allow their fathers larger identities than straight women permit theirs. A matter-of-factness persists in these twenty-seven pieces, a certain acceptance of the paradoxical states in which recklessness and cruelty, tenderness and bumbling, parental love and sexual terror can exist side by side. An evenness of tone is the most unifying aspect, though there is ample evidence of gratitude in the descriptions of playful dads, companion dads, and dads who fill in for missing moms. But there is anger as well, as in Debbra Palmer's poem, along with an urge to retaliate against the father who projects sexual fantasies on his daughter ("and the secrets/ catch up,/ tackle,/ and deep kiss him/ red hair and lipstick everywhere,/ ramming their tongues down his throat/ just the way he/ doesn't/ like it"). Anger blends with distress and confusion for the father who has transgendered, for the daughter who must now deal with this new female body. There is also the critical exposure of a dad who suicides, and a child's stunned disbelief of a dad who kills.

I argue, too, that we won't be caught as often in an inability to express anger at our fathers because of our basic exemption from the classic oedipal triangle, in which every young girl supposedly shifts her desire from her mother to her father as she matures. According to this theory, when differentiation begins (*I look like my mother and she has little power, but Oh, then there's Dad, with his penis and his status*), a rivalry is born, and Dad becomes the adored one until another man takes his place.

But as most of us have noticed, this psychological model holds little truth for lesbians. For us, this mother-father dance marks the beginning of our transgressions, the place we claim that is unlike either of them. We absorb plenty of lessons from our mothers (as portrayed in *Every Woman*), and glean from our fathers what we need to know about access and currency, power and privilege, how to take the top, take the lead, take our lover where she aches to go. Though as we knowingly or unknowingly examine what each sex offers, it's common sense as much as queerness that ultimately prevails, as V. Hunt describes in "Cheaters at the Wedding":

> My mother tried to . . . distract me with expensive new dresses and a Barbie with her own set of wheels. She tried to point out subtle advantages to being a girl–bright colored sweaters, purses full of trinkets, men who'd give you a half dollar for a smile and a curtsey, but I wasn't convinced. Maybe I missed some Freudian stage . . . or maybe I just looked around and noticed that guys got a better deal. Boys could make money. They could mow lawns and have paper routes. They had sports equipment–helmets, pads, masks, gloves; uniforms. And they could get girls to wait on them. With just a kind word, a compliment, a you-sure-look-pretty-in-that-color, guys could get girls to bring them a Coke, finish a raking job, or run in the house and get them some gum. My sisters were perfect examples.

Hunt's pleasure in the obvious–who wouldn't want to be a boy?–is characteristic of a distinct difference between the writings on mothers and this current collection on fathers. In *Every Woman*, a number of writers admitted to feeling stung or irritated when a mother wanted some other identity for herself besides that of parent–when she pursued being a potter, a performer, an activist, an athlete, a lover of sex and sexual pleasure. In describing fathers, however, many of the writers delight in what is quirky or unique about him, their sentences quicker and more buoyant whenever he acts out of type or does something odd or irreverent. ("Having two wives at the same time," writes Jewelle Gomez, "did seem unusual to me when I was a kid, but it never seemed unnatural in my father.") We seem to cut Dad more slack than we do Mom; he can be mischievous, unfaithful, inappropriate, and, more often than not, we see these acts as endearing.

A "big brother," says Christian McEwen, "our rebel emperor." "He was a child like my brothers and sister and me," writes Lu Vickers, "as astonished at the natural world as we were." He is transparent, as when Sheila Ortiz Taylor beats her father in a game of hearts: "In defeating him, I moved into his camp. At the age of nine, I had been initiated into the world of power. . . . We were equals, partners in an apparently genderless world." He is impulsive, as when V. Hunt's father chooses his middle daughter to be his son: "[He] threw the football with me, shot baskets, bought me high-top sneakers, and taught me how to tie a Windsor knot in a tie. All things I think he regretted when I came out. 'It's my fault,' he said. 'Your mother warned me about letting you wear that tie.' "

In this adolescent state, there is a distinct bliss in being chosen, tapped by Dad to enter this rough-and-tumble male world. "I was his son," adds McEwen, "his acolyte, his page boy. In a parallel story, which was somehow just as true, I also felt completely free and genderless." He is "my true comrade," writes Linda Smukler, conflating father and daughter into all the good male roles in "Lover Father Son."

For others, there is the anguish at having been tapped, but not doing it well enough, as in Karin Cook's sense of being invisible to her triathlete father. She takes up distance running in "the hope, perhaps, that if I donned the neon lycra and reflector panels, he would finally see me." Yet he can't stay to watch her complete her first New York City Marathon; he has overestimated her pace, oblivious to her speed and process, and has to hurry on when she is still miles from the finish line. For Gretchen Legler, fly fishing as a girl was a way to be close to her father, a Fishergirl identity she eagerly assumed, "never imagining that later, as a grown woman, the teaching would begin to feel like a molding." She finishes graduate school; comes out as a lesbian and divorces her husband; takes a teaching position in Alaska; and remains so invisible to her father, other than as his fishing daughter, that she wants to smother the competent Fishergirl, "and even suffer the damage I do to myself in the process, all to finally wreck this rickety bridge that joins us, to wipe away this part of me that feels so made by him."

For other writers, adolescence opens a rift with Dad, a hormonal rush that has nothing to do with a desire to separate or be different from him. "I feel my father move back from this fecund wave," writes Helena Lipstadt in her prose poem "Tzimtzum." "[T]he curving billowing female space of his daughter emitting the smell of sex. I don't want him to withdraw, to lose him, I want him to let me change into a woman, tell me he approves of my beauty and my heat. . . . He leaves me anyway and I am left carrying his confusion and horror. Braid and twist and iron and still perfume the room with the unbridled smell of me."

"The last time he touched me without thinking first," writes Minnie Bruce Pratt, "he held my hand, I was three or four, and I was his. He tipped his panama hat to everyone he met as they admired his baby, too young to be a girl, who twirled on the lunch counter stool while his buddies fed her ice cream." "I presented him with no rivals," writes Holly Iglesias, sensing that her father might retreat from any evidence of her developing body.

I didn't date in high school. You could say I wasn't interested; you could say I was a nerd or that I was queer. Each one bears a partial truth, but what matters is that I thought I was sexless. I know that this helped to ease tensions between my dad and me when I was a teenager, because he treated my sister, who was most definitely interested in boys, quite differently–with a disconcerting blend of awe and panic.

Unfortunately, entering adulthood brings a wider vision, a larger context for questions of inheritance, of gene-linked traits and frightening patterns. "My father could trace some of his bloodlines across the ocean to England," writes Bia Lowe in "Blood," "a heritage he played to the hilt, a fantasy of landed gentry, with his brood of hunting dogs, his collection of guns, a fondness for organ meats and hard liquor. . . . I knew at a young age that alcohol would claim a chunk of my legacy." Genetic predisposition haunts Christian McEwen's life, too, with the twin threats of manic depression and alcoholism. Laura Markowitz prepared to be an orphan after her mother dies and her father's grief makes him transparent, "a flawed human being. . . . I expected the car crash, the mugger, the heart attack, as I stood waiting for him to come home from work. I . . . raged at him for abandoning me, even though he was the one who lived."

Yet witnessing a father's frailty, his terrible, undeniable human-ness, brings many of these daughters home, as they sit with him through brutal illnesses, or are present when he dies. For Holly Hughes, news of her father's cancer brings with it another awful conflict: "When sickness enters one person's body, it doesn't just stay there. It comes to live with everyone who loves that body, its appearance determined by the kind of love you have for the body where the sickness makes its home . . . Fuck! I didn't just say I loved my father, did I? I meant to imply I loved his *body*. Which is not *him*. My *father*, his *body* . . . two completely separate entities. Barely on speaking terms."

"I *see* them digging into you," writes Carol Potter in "By-Pass," envisioning her father on the operating table,

parting bone from bone–
they lay you open like a furrow.

I am certain they will find
a cluster of words
huddled in your veins,
a gang of shouting children
flocked in your blood.

"You think about the body, this delicate machine," writes Cheryl B., of the hours at her dying father's bedside. "[T]he aspirations of a Florida retirement, a life spent in overtime, waiting; how he gambled his soul on a dream he was fed like corn flakes and ended up with nothing but a coffee can full of OTB winnings and a body full of cancer. . . . You want to tell him you would rewrite his life if you could."

Yet, despite the grief recorded here; despite the brutality and violence; despite the flaws and the stumbling, a big embrace of Dad comes through, a love of his hands, his tools, his sex, his dress. In Holly Hughes' case, a love of "his shotguns. His poison. The big sign he made, black letters on white wood: Private Property. Keep Out. Out of the corner of my eyes, I studied his hands. Massive. Like paws. The big hands of a hard worker. He was always working, so I could walk barefoot under the pines. Through our woods."

"You look just like your father," says Peggy Shaw's mother. "Do you know you look just like your father? You remind me of him. Do you want a pair of his cuff links? I know where they are. How about a tie? I have one of his summer ties. Oh, how you remind me of him when he was a young farmer, he had those muscles in his forearms that stuck out from milking cows." Shaw's response to this heavy flirtation: "I dressed in my mother's memories. . . . I shined my shoes while they were on, and my mother smiled. 'You look just like your father,' she said. I think she wanted me to kiss her hand."

"My father was my femme top role model," writes Tristan Taormino. "My father made me the girl I am today–one who likes anonymous sex, showtunes, and well-dressed men. Not to mention butchy girlfags, Bette Midler, and leather. . . . And I do love dykes who are daddies. Fierce butch tops with slick, shiny, barbershop haircuts and shirts that button the other way. Daddies who have dicks made of flesh and silicone and latex and magic. Daddies with hands that touch me like they have been touching my body their entire lives. Daddies who have big cocks, love blow-jobs, and like to fuck girls hard."

*   *   *

I have spent several years now paying particularly attention to the treatment of dads, and I find one of the oddest to be the current image in movies and commercials of "Mr. Mom," of "Dad-as-Mom," of Dad doing the job even better than Mom, despite all the evidence to the contrary.

I have asked university students about it, during discussions about gender roles during literature classes. I want to know if they see any implied insult to men in such a characterization, that calling him a "mother" shortchanges his father potential. The students, however, resist this quite adamantly, not wanting to tarnish their idea of "Dad," not wanting "Father" to include softness or diaper-changing or pumped-milk bottle feedings. Those activities, they insist, are exceptions done out of a love, a lofty sense of cooperation, done by a dad sitting in for a mom, not a multi-faceted, complex Dad, who could build bridges, sell stocks, load boats, grill burgers and also find a moment to dry and powder the smallest squawler. "Father," they want me to know, without saying so directly, must remain synonymous with Power and Order. Nothing of the female should permeate that image, weakening its knees, softening its muscle. I point out the lack of a similar label for women, a "Mom-as-Dad" identity, but most won't be tricked or fall for the traps. The phrase "Dad-as-Mom" works because it maintains a necessary masculine core, neither prettified nor sullied simply for nurturing a dependent.

Their resistance reminds me of the dangers of a two-gendered system, and I'm grateful once again for the places we can go as lesbians, straddling rules and roles and choices. One of the clear messages of this collection is that, by examining and challenging the traditional images, not only are we able to accept Dad's whole self, his skills and his shortcomings, but we also accept the parts of him that we've adopted, whether consciously or not. As Audre Lorde writes in her Prologue to Zami: A New Spelling of My Name, "I have always wanted to be both man and woman, to incorporate the strongest and richest parts of my mother and father within/into me–to share valleys and mountains upon my body the way the earth does in hills and peaks. I would like to enter a woman the way any man can, and to be entered–to leave and to be left–to be hot and hard and soft all at the same time in the cause of our loving."

Catherine Reid
January 2000

Lover Brother Son

Linda Smukler

My daughter could have been my son   a young boy with a crew cut and a t-shirt and little shorts   a few brown-blonde curls at the nape of his neck   I raise him alone   protect and care for him   this is my boy who is going to be tall and has a great catch   mitt held high   a good throw too   we dress the same and he pleases me beyond anything I know   later he will join me in my medical practice and I am the kind of father to him that my father never was to me   I listen and do not impose my will   then again he will be a poet and I will be a poet along with him   he will take care of me when I am old and I will hold his children or I will hold him because he is also my brother   my true comrade   the best man at my wedding   my brother does not drink or get angry   he is not embittered   he loves our mother despite her needs and diffuses our father's rage   my brother takes my hand and helps me cross the street   he teaches me to ride a two-wheel bike and reads to me on the grasses above Delphi   he is my lover too   he brings me berries and helps me plant my garden   architects together living in a home designed and built by our own hands   he travels with me on an Alaskan journey to study puffins   he and the sky are more than either of us can bear   the azure blue   the beauty of it all   we will cry together and not be ashamed   he is present at the birth of my first son   whom I name after him   even though as Jews it is forbidden to name after the living   only the dead

Cheaters at the Wedding

V. Hunt

My dad plays it casual, cool, a wry smile when I ask about his new air-brushed license plate–*The Legend*–in smoky script, affixed below the car's elaborate grill. He reaches into the dove-gray leather console of the Cadillac Seville and pulls out a cassette. "Let me play you a tape somebody made me," he says. It's an answer, I know, to my question. Stevie Nicks comes on singing, "You could be my silver spring."

He's just picked me up from the airport. I've flown home–alone–for my brother's wedding. "Laura couldn't make it?" my dad asks, lowering the volume. As he reaches for the knob, I notice a twine bracelet with several tiny black beads almost hidden beneath his watch.

"Busy at work," I say, shrugging, trying to act like it's no big deal. Laura and I have been together eighteen years; it's been a long time since I've been anywhere without her, especially home. "You wearing bracelets now?" I ask, nodding toward his wrist. He pushes the beads back beneath his bulky metal watchband.

"It's some kind of a luck thing," he says. "Once it's on there you gotta wait for it to wear itself off."

"Next thing I know you'll have your ear pierced."

My father rolls his eyes toward me. "Being a smartass don't become you," he says. He's hoping that will change the subject. I just smile, and he begins to fidget with his hair, combing his fingers nervously, almost womanly, through the thin pieces on top. I've never seen his hair so long. He retired from the Army years ago, but has always kept it regulation short. Now, despite the scalp poking through at the crown, the sides are bushier and the back isn't shaved as high. It's darker, too, but he's been experimenting

15

with get-out-the-gray formulas for years. The tape changes to a new song and Bonnie Raitt comes on, singing, "I Can't Make You Love Me."

"I like this song," I say. "Now who'd you say made this tape? I thought you were all George Jones and Reba McEntire."

He smiles. "You don't know her," he says, and rubs his palms down his thighs, as if to dry his hands. The worn white creases in his jeans, ironed in with military precision, barely flatten beneath the pressure.

We drive down Kingston Pike listening to the music. Now that I'm older I can finally see what others have always told me. No DNA tests needed; we're cut from the same piece of cloth. We've got the same unmistakably large nose, coarse hair, wavy when it gets too long, more freckles than anybody can count. But it's more than our looks; we're both cocky, assured, confident to a danger- ous degree. When I was a kid, if I ran inside to tell my father that I'd been pushed down, he'd say, "So. When someone pushes me, that's my problem. When someone pushes you, that's yours. Go push him back." I did. "Don't start fights," my dad always said, "just finish them." I do.

He never suggested that, as a girl, I should act differently than boys. Like most young soldiers, he had wanted a son, expected one, when my older sister was born. A few years later, when I came along, he was, like any father, delighted in my strong lungs, my dark red hair, my early swagger, but still disappointed in not having a boy. When one more try resulted in one more girl, well, it seemed time to go to Plan B. After all, his marriage to my mother was already shaky. He was downing beers at the bar each night until he knew the girls were asleep, while my mother took diet pills for her figure and birth control pills for everything else. Three girls would have to do. So my father picked, and I was chosen. I would be his son.

My mother tried to talk me out of it, to distract me with expensive new dresses and a Barbie with her own set of wheels. She tried to point out subtle advantages to being a girl—bright colored sweaters, purses full of trinkets, men who'd give you a half dollar for a smile and a curtsey, but I wasn't convinced. Maybe I missed some Freudian stage, or got stuck in one, or maybe I just looked around and noticed that guys got a better deal. Boys could make money. They could mow lawns and have paper routes. They had sports equipment–helmets, pads, masks, gloves; uniforms. And they could get girls to wait on them. With just a kind word, a compliment, a you-sure-look-pretty-in-that-color, guys could get girls to bring them a Coke, finish a raking job, or run in the house and get them some gum. My sisters were perfect examples.

In the summer, I would go to work with my dad, riding a bicycle through a giant military warehouse, stamping addresses on big pieces of machinery, while my sisters stayed home and cleaned toilets and vacuumed floors. My father threw the football with me, shot baskets, bought me high-top sneakers, and taught me how to tie a Windsor knot in a tie. All things I think he regretted when I came out. "It's my fault," he said. "Your mother warned me about letting you wear that tie."

My mother had warned him about a lot of things to which he paid no attention–her waning interest in him, in us; her need to be more than a thirty-year-old mother of three. But discontent was common among soldiers' wives. None of us thought much of it as she slogged along for several more years, getting her girls raised, getting them old enough, for what, we weren't sure. Then, like a miracle, a curse, she was pregnant again, and this time gave my father his son, a parting gift. When she brought the new boy home, my father never seemed more happy; my mother never seemed more miserable. A week before my brother's second birthday, my mother filed for divorce. Wanting to limit her memories, and short on means of support, she left most things behind, including the kids. She took only a few photographs, some clothes she hadn't fit into for years, and a jewelry case made from a cigar box and painted macaroni that my sister and I had once made as a Mother's Day gift. Maybe if I'd known she would never be back, I would've asked about the swelling around my breasts, about something that had recently ruptured, the trickle of blood I'd found. She left, it seemed, just when my dad and I needed her most.

After the shock wore off, after my sisters had learned how to handle all their new responsibilities, my dad and I both started dating, both looking for someone, anyone, to help us manage. No one was shocked, least of all my father, when, at the age of fifteen, I fell in love with a woman. He didn't approve of my first choice, especially since her husband took it so hard. But he knew, had been knowing, that I would need a woman's help. After several failed attempts at domestic life with one girl or another, he was truly happy for me, breathed a sigh of relief, when I met Laura. Still, when I first came out, my father had tried weakly to talk me out of it. "Girly love," he began, and I can't remember the rest. It was something he'd picked up from being around WACS. Something about the difficulties, the trials and tribulations of trying to love women. He seemed to know what he was talking about. Maybe I should've listened. But now it wasn't advice on loving women that I needed. I'd figured that out pretty well by myself. I needed to know how to cheat.

The tape segued into Mariah Carey's "Dream Lover," a song I'd recently made afternoon love to in a Motel 6 just a few exits down the interstate from my house. That same song was on a tape that my other girlfriend had made for me. I looked over and it seemed like my dad was kind of mouthing the words: *Take me up, take me down, take me any way you want to.*

I stared straight through the windshield. A few yards away was a sign for a bowling alley. "Want to bowl a few games?" I asked. I was on a league, and out-of-town bowling tournaments had proven handy excuses for spending time with my other girlfriend.

He looked over. We both smiled. "They got a million things for us to do," he said.

"Like what?"

"The rehearsal dinner," he said. "Stuff at the fellowship hall."

"Fuck 'em," I said.

He laughed. "You'll get the girls all mad, then I'll have to deal with them." My sisters always complained that I skated through the hard work of slicing and dicing, only showing up to sprinkle on some parsley then wanting credit for the presentation.

"Come on," I said, "it's early. They're going to get stirred up whether we're there or not." We were nearing the bowling alley. He slowed but didn't put on his blinker.

He shook his head. "We shouldn't," he said, speeding up, looking at the bowling alley in his rearview mirror.

"Getting like Robert," I said, the ultimate insult. It was agreed by all that my uncle Robert was PW–pussy-whipped. A more favorable spin was that April, his new young wife, kept him "fucked down." No doubt he'd become a different man since getting a divorce and remarrying. Everybody swore it wouldn't last, even if he was immature and April was thirteen years younger. My dad's latest wife was younger, too, or had been when he married her. She'd aged over the years and seemed somewhat dowdy now. She was content to stay home piecing quilts or making fig preserves while my father went off to car shows. At least that's where he told her he was going.

"I'm telling," he said, slowing the car, preparing to turn around. "I'm telling them that it was all your idea."

Inside, the bowling alley was dark, only a few lanes in use, men who might've slipped off from work a little early but weren't ready to go home, or maybe divorcés with no place else to go. They barely looked up when we entered, intent on their rhythm, their scores. Behind the counter, a large man was reading a tabloid, *The Weekly World News*, an article about a man with a one-inch penis. There was a full-page picture of the poor guy standing nude beneath the caption, his hands delicately crossed to cover his crotch. On the facing page was a picture of him standing next to his smiling wife and several smiling children. The counter man set the paper aside with a grunt, sprayed anti-fungal in the shoes we rented, and pointed us to a lane on the far side of the alley, away from the men already bowling. We looked through the racks of balls, trying to find the right weight, the right fit. I bought us a pitcher of beer and we settled into our lane.

We hadn't bowled together in years. We hadn't done anything together in years. I only went home regularly for Christmas nowadays, or for a special occasion, and always with Laura, always with a long list of places to go and people to see. My father and I rarely even found time for a drink together anymore. So it seemed fun to be bowling together in the middle of the afternoon when we were supposed to be somewhere else.

Our rhythm was awkward through the first few frames. After missing a couple of easy spares, I took off the vest and bolo tie I'd worn on the plane, and rolled up my shirt sleeves to get more comfortable. My father went back to look for a different ball. His knuckles were knotty in places from arthritis, so he needed one with large holes. I noticed him wince sometimes as he gripped the ball. "You okay?" I asked.

"Yeah, yeah, I'm fine," he answered. "A little stiff." I couldn't help noticing the loose skin on his arms. Even in winter, he wore short sleeves, cuffed up a turn or two, a habit he'd developed to show off what had once been well-shaped biceps.

We didn't talk much through the first game except to complain about the lanes, the warped spots in the floor, our tendency for nailing the head-pin, all the splits. In the end, I beat him by twelve pins. I went for a second pitcher of beer while he hunted for another ball, maybe one a little lighter.

During the second game we were looser, rolling the ball hard, delighting in the pin action, even on misfires. We high-fived each other over unlikely pick-ups. I drained the second pitcher as my dad rolled three straight strikes to win. "One more," I said, waving the empty container. We were both feeling the effects of the beer, but it was part of the game. The next would be won or lost under tougher conditions, or maybe neither one of us would give a damn. We both seemed ready to give in. There were things I wanted to talk about, things more important than strikes and splits.

"Hard to believe Scott's getting married," I said. We were bowling slower now, taking more time between each turn.

My father reached behind him for his beer cup, took a sip, and shook his head. "Hope he knows what he's doing," he said.

"She seems nice, a good family and all."

"I reckon," he said, "but don't seem like Scott's sowed all the oats he should've by now. Know what I mean?"

I nodded and shrugged, drying my hands on the blower as I waited for my ball to return. "Everybody's different," I said.

"Not you and me," he said, absently poking the string bracelet back beneath his watchband.

I smiled, turned and rolled my ball down the lane, picking up the pins I'd left.

"Maybe he's smarter than us," I said, coming back to the seat beside him. "Maybe he knows how to keep it all working."

My dad reached back for his beer cup again. "Nah," he said, "it's like this beer here. See them bubbles?" He nodded toward the small streak of foam at the top of his cup. "That's what makes beer good. But they don't last. Just watch it. Don't matter what you do, they bubble up, then pop and go flat."

I didn't want to talk about beer. I wanted to talk about secluded parks where no one was watching as my hands roamed over and underneath, about little restaurants with pricey menus, romantic even at lunch. I wanted to know how to get the flush out of my face and the tingle from between my legs when it was time to go home. I wanted to know how to do it and not feel guilty.

I looked at the beer he was holding, then at my own, almost empty, the bubbles gone. "Well, you just get you another one then," I said. "One that isn't flat."

"That's right," he said, looking up at me. "That's what most of us do." He got up to bowl while I poured me another beer, splashing it into the cup, urging it up to a head. I stared at the foam popping against the rim, looking hard as if it might contain some message.

We bowled the last few frames in silence, tired now, a little past drunk. We both missed several easy pick-ups, but only shrugged as our ball sailed silently by the pins and clunked into the return. I won, but not on a score to brag about. We took off our shoes slowly. Somber now, as if we'd pulled back the curtain on something we'd rather not have seen.

"Want this last beer?" I asked, sloshing the last few inches around the bottom of the pitcher.

"Better not," my dad said. "We've got enough explaining to do."

There was a whirl of activity at the house. My sisters had never really gotten along with Betty, my dad's latest wife, and the friction intensified whenever they all got tangled in the same kitchen. One of my sisters was fretting over some sausage pinwheels that didn't seem to be rising. The red cabbage leaves, which had looked so pretty holding the various kinds of dip in the recipe cut from a magazine, looked droopy and sloppy as a centerpiece. Betty had burned the peanuts and the Chex mix tasted scorched. And as if all that weren't enough, my brother had waited until just now to tell my sister that she couldn't use champagne as dressing for her fruit salad because of his wife being a Baptist. My father simply strolled past the kitchen complaints, settled into his La-Z-Boy chair, clicked the remote until he found a war movie on TBS, then fell into a beer-induced doze.

No one seemed to notice or care that we'd been gone too long. Over and over I assured everyone that Laura was all right; no, we weren't having problems; just busy, a lot going on with her job; she sends her best, sorry she couldn't make it. My brother seemed the most disappointed. "She should be here," he said. "You know, for the family pictures. The ones with everybody."

"She wanted to, just couldn't right now," I said, thinking of the fight we'd had before I left. I had begged her to come with me. "Think how it will look," I said. "You've gotta do this for me, for my family. They'll freak, ask me a million questions. If you're not there, they'll know."

"Well, you're good at lying," she said. "You'll think of some-thing."

"They'll be crushed," I said. "They'll be disappointed."

"Just tell them you're a chip off the old block," she said. "They'll get it." Despite my pleading, she was adamant in her refusal but did offer to shop for a new outfit I could wear to the wedding. While I wandered in electronics and sporting goods, she scanned the racks in women's wear, wanting me to have something nice, something new, something I'd look good in, and the right kind of shoes. The night before I left, she arranged my clothes carefully–packaged soap, toothpaste, deodorant, and cologne–and tucked everything solemnly into a suitcase, like a wife packing for her traveling spouse who she knows takes off his wedding ring on the ride to the airport.

I carried my suitcase in from the car. "I wanted you for best man," my brother said, following me down the hall and into the guest room. "I had it all planned, a tux and everything. But Tammy said the bridesmaid that had to walk up there with you would feel funny about it."

"It's OK," I said. "I appreciate the thought." Actually that would've been great, perfect. I had agonized for weeks, finally trusting Laura's decision over the appropriate thing to wear.

"I guess it's weird," he said. "But it's like we're brothers, you know. I mean, I've even got that same bad loop in my golf swing." He laughed, trying not to get too sentimental. It'd been a long week and it showed in the circles beneath his eyes. He flopped down wearily on the bed where I'd thrown my suitcase. There was an old quilt as a bedspread, a crazy quilt made without a pattern from whatever scraps could be found. He traced his finger over one of the patches, a blue plaid flannel that had probably been his pajamas. He stared up at the ceiling as I started pulling out clothes that I needed to hang up before they got more wrinkled. He rubbed his hands over his face, lingering near his eyes, trying to push back tears that seemed to keep gathering there.

"I've warned you about taking up my ways," I said. "Cause you nothing but trouble."

"But you've done it right," he said, raising up on his elbows. "I mean, in love. I told Tammy, 'That's what I want, what they've got.' I mean the way y'all are, the way you've been so long." He looked toward me like I should tell him now, the secret, the words of wisdom that would make his marriage last in a family prone to divorce.

"There's been ups and downs," I said.

"Sure," he said, "I know, and just look at you."

Yeah, I wanted to say, just look at me. Look at someone who hides credit card receipts for wine-drenched lunches and back-of-the-lot motel rooms; who checks the car upholstery for stray blonde hairs, and buries tapes full of sexy songs in the bottom of the console. Look at someone who dreams up lies about the time that got away; who parks the car in the driveway, gives the old lady a kiss with just-brushed teeth, and calmly complains that there's too much salt in the potatoes. I wanted to scream: For god's sake, don't be like me, like any of us.

"I mean, I could ask Dad," he continued, flopping back, looking up at some invisible message on the ceiling. "But you know his track record." He waited for my response, and when there wasn't one, he rolled to his side and watched as I pulled out the conservative, smartly tailored, navy blue dress with a vest that Laura had bought for me to wear to the wedding. "Wow, you're wearing a dress?" My brother stared at the garment as if it were some brightly colored tribal costume.

"When in Rome," I said.

"The whole world's gone crazy," my brother said, sitting up and shaking his head. "I hope it's not some kind of sign or something."

I wanted to stop his shaking head. I wanted to tell him everything, how easy it is to fail, to disappoint. Tell him about the look on Laura's face when she found the letters, the cards, the pictures I thought were well hidden in my desk. I wanted to talk to him like a sister, like a woman. I wanted him to hold me while I cried.

My brother sat on the edge of the bed, pale, looking washed out against the swirl of colors in the quilt. He was waiting.

"You've picked a good girl," I said, saying what I knew he wanted to hear. "You're going to have a good marriage."

He smiled, looked at me hard, trying to see if I was lying, joking; if there was sarcasm in my eyes. I looked back as sincerely as I could, the steady gaze of a brother. Satisfied, he said, "I can't believe you're going to wear a dress."

"Aren't you supposed to be somewhere practicing vows or something?" I asked, pushing him off the bed.

At the wedding, there was something dark about the church in spite of the bright poinsettias. A December wedding, Christmas plaid the featured color. The black, white and red blends of bows and cummerbunds made a bouncy contrast to the polished pine of the country church, but it all seemed falsely cheerful against the sheets of rain falling outside. As we waited for the ceremony to begin, a male-and-female duet sang hymns and Christmas songs to a karaoke machine. I looked around, almost wishing my mother would come busting down the aisle, dressed to the nines, and assume her place in the mother's pew. But no, even though invited, my mother wouldn't come. It had been over twenty-five years since she left. Perhaps we wouldn't even recognize her. She was the only notable absence; otherwise, the church was packed. Ushers escorted old ladies down the aisle, including my great-aunt Mamie, who everyone said had been my grandfather's mistress. The story goes that he couldn't decide between the sisters, so he married one and moved the other up the hill. She sat with the other widow women, a solid block about halfway back. Finally, the organ music started, the ceremony began. My father, the second choice, served as best man. My sisters cried uncontrollably. They dabbed wadded tissues around their eyes, trying not to ruin the make-up they'd spent hours applying. Mascara-free, I could've cried all I wanted. But I held up, brother-like, in spite of my dress.

My dad stood at the edge of the altar like a sentinel, his eyes focused on some unseen object on the horizon, his shoulders squared, his thumbs in line with the seams of his trousers. There was a drop of sweat dangling from his nose, but standing at attention, he wouldn't wipe it. He'd gotten a haircut that morning, and there was something boyish in the clean razor lines above his ears, the crisp height of the tux collar. I looked, but couldn't tell if he was still wearing the string bracelet with the lucky beads. It was a rented tux, and the sleeves fell a bit long in the cuff. When the preacher shifted the bride and groom toward the center, my father used the opportunity to quickly mop the moisture from his face with a clean white handkerchief. A calm fell over the church as my brother began the solemn recitation of his vows. His voice was strong, full of conviction. There was no doubt. He believed in this love, this marriage. As my brother kissed his new bride, my father pulled out his handkerchief again and put it up to his eyes, catching a tear before it could roll down his face. I reached for the tiny blue clutch bag Laura had sent along, "just in case," and pulled out the hanky folded inside, allowing one small sob for all of us.

from *You're Just Like My Father*

Peggy Shaw

(Lights come up on Peggy, sitting on a chair on a bare stage with bare breasts and boxer shorts, bare feet. She wraps her breasts with an ace bandage and goes over to a suitcase on a table and opens it . . . She gets another bandage from the suitcase and wraps on top of the first bandage. She removes the hand boxing wrap and wraps a hand . . . When she is finished wrapping, she drops her head into her hands and growls like a wolf.)

The landlord wouldn't fix the toilet
'Cause he said there was nothing wrong with it.
She didn't know what she was planning on doing
She knew she had to do something.
You get no satisfaction calling in the authorities.
She watched the darkness in her window, waiting for some kind
Of release, but nothing came.
Her arms needed to strike out, to drive outside of her what was
Eating her up inside, but there was always such consequences in
Wrecking a place to feel better.
She went over to the Kleenex box on the shelf, and started tearing
Up white pieces of Kleenex into tiny white squares,
Then she filled each square with a little pile of white sugar.
Then she drew up the Kleenex in a little sack
And tied each one with a piece of string.
This took her all afternoon.
She waited until she knew it would rain and spread her tiny bundles
All over the big, beautiful, groomed, green lawn in front of his office.
It rained good and hard.
The next day the big, beautiful, groomed, green lawn was dotted with

Hundreds of white specks of sugar stuck to the blades of grass.
There were no complaints to the management or to the police.
Only to the minister.
And the minister went to speak to the family, to her husband.
But since he was dead, he couldn't take the blame.
That is to say, my father couldn't take the blame.
'Cause this was my mother before they destroyed her.
My mother who was in love with me in the house.

(Runs hands through hair, making sound of a wolf. Fade to black.)
Hey!
I'm Eddie.
My father wouldn't call me Eddie, he called me Margaret.
Margaret means pearl.
I was his pearl of a girl.
But pearl didn't match my outfits.
This is my face. It's sharp and I look like my father.
You look just like your father, my mother would say.
I look like my father when I'm in a good mood.
Most lesbians I know really like their father, me included.
My father was a Leo, he had a heart condition; he had to count to
   ten before he hit us.
He gave me the same heart condition simply because I knew him
   so well.
He had big hands. I have his big hands.
I like to touch things and people. Once a shrink asked me where my
Desire comes from.
I said, "From my hands."
She told me to keep my hands to myself. She didn't mean to say it.
It just came out and embarrassed her.
I guess shrinks aren't supposed to be so direct.
But I knew what she meant.
There were so many children in my family that when we visited
People's houses we all had to hold our hands behind our backs
For the whole visit so

We couldn't touch anything.

I have to control my hands all the time.

My grandmother told me I would do great things with my hands; I think

She meant play the piano.

My father told me that his father knocked out Joe Louis with his bare

Hands.

(Musical number: "This is a man's world." During all musical numbers a microphone descends from ceiling as in a boxing ring.)

As hard

As I've tried

I can't get it up

Fully

On top

You know

Head

To toe

Missionary

Go tell it on the mountain

But mounting

Is something I've got trouble with

'Cause I can't

Get on top

Get hard

Butch on top

It's left over

From way back

When I was a boy

And all the girls

Wanted me to please

It's hard
To keep it up
My reputation
Easy for the young ones
But hard for me
But not hard enough.
If it only comes down
Or comes up
To coming
To keep it going
To keep it up
To strapping one on
To whacking me off
'Cause
Deep inside my love for you
Is a flash picture
It has to do with my arms
My fingers
My hands
These are the butch queer feminine parts
Of me
On the other hand
Either my left or my right
I'm told that I'm missing out on a dildo.
I can hardly look at the real ones
That look like real dicks
I can look at the dolphin ones
Dolphins don't have veins.
It's the veins.
That vanity in men.
I think Moby Dick was really a dolphin.
My father's dick looked like a dolphin
When I saw him
In the toilet.
Feminists made me hate dolphins, I mean dildos.

They tried to make me hate boxer shorts
Not that I want to put blame
On anyone for my
Lack of thrust
Except maybe the missionaries.
I don't want to be like my parents
In any way
Unless, of course,
I can't help it
You should never take your parents personally.

[. . .]
(Traveling music such as in Pee Wee's Big Top.)

I always pack a gun.
That gives me the I'm-OK-you're-OK look.
The one I use for borders.
Sometimes it works for me.
Once I went through a border with a drag queen, who was
    dressed butch
To pass as a man.
I was dressed femme to pass as a girl.
They pulled us over and wanted to see our suitcases.
He got my suitcase with suits and ties and letters to girls.
And I got his suitcase, with dresses and high heels and poems to boys.
They passed us through as normal.
But I didn't have my gun.
And I didn't have my dildo.
Packing, I call it, in both cases.
I carry my gun, unlike my dildo.
I carry it just in case.
The gun, that is. I keep the dildo in my drawers with my neatly
    folded
White boxer shorts.

I don't use it. I'm not dangerous.
Knowing I'm safe makes me a trustworthy person.
You could even trust me with your wife if you wanted to.

(Spit.)
She told me she loved the name Peggy, it was a beautiful name.
The first, sweetest thing any girl ever told me was that she
Was at a drive-in movie with her boyfriend Paul
And while they were making out she had whispered my
Name by mistake, and Paul drove her right home
And threw up all over her lawn. It filled me with fear and
Power at the same time. The fear came from being caught
For the pervert that I was.
The power came from the effect it had on the lawn.
I always associate wrecking lawns with power. *(Spit.)*
Everytime someone hurts me, I want to become famous
And buy a 1962 Corvette and get all dressed up
With a beautiful woman next to me,
And drive past them on the street,
Just so they can catch a glimpse of me
And how happy and successful I am.
I got that from Jimmy Cagney.

(Rock and roll music such as "Stick Shift.")
I associate everything with cars, except my sexuality I attribute to
my hands. The only thing I liked about *Desert Hearts* was when
she went backwards really fast in her truck.

(Rock and roll music continues under monologue.)
I got really excited when I realized that my sexuality was also in
my lips. I got that from Elvis Presley. He taught me to pay
attention to my lips. I would try to sneer like him when flirting
with girls, and that's when I developed the habit of licking my lips,

to keep them moist and desirable. I felt like people were staring at my lips at a time when most girls thought people were staring at their breasts. Sometimes I had to cover my lips with my hands because they felt vulnerable and naked, and dangerous and out of control. I used to pretend that my hand, that soft part between the index finger and the thumb, was Marie Manjouritis's lips. And I would kiss that part of my hand and put my tongue through the opening. I would feel embarrassed when I saw her because I thought that she would remember how passionate my kiss was and tell someone and put me in sex jail.

The man I am today still thinks all desire starts at the mouth. It comes from right inside the lip, the inside part of the lips that are always moist.

(Fade music.)
The only part of getting old that I worry about is that my lips will dry up and be hard and wrinkly, and that thought's enough to break me into a sweat in the middle of day, let alone the middle of the night.

Meanwhile, my mother was watching and flirting with me.

(Hands over face, sound of wolf as in beginning.)
(Blood pressure machine put on arm.)
I went into the subway at West Fourth Street in the summer, and came out in Brooklyn in the fall. That's how fast time is moving, moving along with my blood. My blood is trying to tell me something, clotting up and trying to torture me so it can get out of me, moving through me in blood clots of magnitude. My blood is a volcano. I met the goddess Pele at the volcano. I offered my body as a sacrifice to Pele, a butch girl sacrifice. Pele likes butches and prefers eating them to almost anyone else. Nice to have a goddess who prefers you. Like Pele, I have high blood pressure. My acupuncturist, who thinks he's Tom Jones, is trying to lower my fire so I won't burn myself up. But I'm afraid that the combination

of that and menopause will make me a boring person. What would a volcano be without her lava? Without her blood?

When I see blood, I want to eat it, chew it up good, or chop it up with onions for chopped liver, put an egg over it and have steak tartare, salt and pepper and some Worcestershire sauce, put it in a blender and add ice for a nice summer drink, a cranberry blood clot or a bloody Mary, but Mary's not here to hold back my hands. I'm down in Pele, reaching for her womb, keep my hands to myself. Keep these big, old, cow-milking, queer hands to myself. Let them hang at my side or behind my back, or slip into my own pants and stay there. Big old hands that want to get sucked into you, sliding uncontrollably up into you, too big to get in, like a newborn baby, ready for the womb, but not the world.

(Testimony.)
(Femme walk to suitcase, starts dressing in a suit.)

My mother used to watch me getting dressed.
I used to let myself take forever getting dressed.
My mother watched me.
She loved me, my mother.
She recognized me.
"You look just like your father," she said.
I put on a starched shirt
And I was my father.
I loved how my father's few Sunday shirts
Looked and smelled when they came back
From the Chinese laundry,
And had a piece of cardboard inside
To keep them rectangular and stiff.
Very stiff and starched.
They had peach-colored bands around them
Keeping all the long sleeves,
And tail tucked in.

When he unfolded his white shirt Sunday morning
It kept its rectangular shapes
All over the sleeves and the cuffs.
And the cuffs were huge and flat and spreading
Out at the bottom of the sleeve
'Cause it hadn't been folded for cuff links.
I wanted to have a starched white shirt like his,
Keeping it safe all week,
Knowing it's in a drawer piled on top of other shirts
And the white folded boxer shorts.
Men's underwear folds so neatly and square,
Women's underwear doesn't have a real logic to it.
And my father had this great gesture after he shaved
Of patting his cheeks with cologne
And running his hands all around his face.
When I touched my own face like that, in a kind of
Rough way, my mother would say,
"Don't touch your face like that, you'll wreck your skin."
But she liked my father's leathery skin
And the way he was pulling up his chin
The whole church service, away from the starched shirt collar.
My mother always held his hand in church,
And seemed fragile, like she would break
If my father's white shirt wasn't there
Keeping the world from caving her in,
Just the idea of the world could cave in my mother.
That's why I chose to be a boy.
So I could wear starched shirts
To keep the ugly world away from girls,
And so girls could hold my hand
And rest their head on my shoulder,
My clean white shoulder, stiff with pleasure.

(Sings crooner song like "To All the Girls I've Loved Before" in the audience.)

[. . .]

"Do you know you look just like your father? You remind me of
him. Do you want a pair of his cuff links? I know where they are.
How about a tie? I have one of his summer ties. Oh, how you
remind me of him when he was a young farmer, he had those
muscles in his forearms that stuck out from milking cows."

And she remembered him. I dressed in my mother's memories.
"But don't let your sisters see you, you know how they copy you,
I don't want them dressing like that, and I worry about you, that
you're going to hell because of the way you dress, eternal hell to
burn with the devil. And I don't want you bringing your sisters with
you."

(Sentimental song like "I'm Confessing That I Love You.")
I shined my shoes while they were on, and my mother smiled.
"You look just like your father," she said. I think she wanted me to
kiss her hand. I put on my hat to leave and the spell was broken.
She forgot who I was, she forgot I was her Sunday lover, and she
said I would burn in hell. I let myself take forever getting dressed.
My mother loved me. She recognized me.

*(Salute and leave with suitcase; song continues through curtain
call.)*

A Dad Called Mama

Lu Vickers

1968

On Sundays my father does not linger in front of the First Baptist Church in Chattahoochee like some people. As soon as he steps outside the big white doors, he jerks his tie loose, lights a cigarette, then herds my brothers and sister and me down the sidewalk to the Plymouth where we wait for Mama so he can drive us home. Walking into the house, he shucks his suit and finishes up cooking the Sunday dinner he started before we left the house that morning. Sometimes, after dinner, he and I drive out to his office where he works on his bug collection. I am nine years old, the only child of his patient enough to indulge him on these sleepy Sunday afternoons.

He sits across from me in his dusty office pressing the crackly bodies of insects into soft wads of cotton lining a shallow wooden box. Pale sunlight washes into the room. On a coal black Smith Corona, he types with two fingers the insects' Latin names onto thin white paper: *Photinus pyralis, Bombus pennsylvanicus.* Those are the same two fingers and the same typewriter on which he will type my essay on Virginia Woolf years later, because I will have refused to learn how to type, think if I do learn how, it will doom me to a life of secretarial work. Little do I know.

He pulls the paper from the typewriter, then cuts it into strips, dabs a bit of glue onto these and places them next to the insects. Then he lowers a plate of glass over the bugs and bends forward, admiring his work. He likes to gaze at these bugs, tells me the exact spot of shade in the woods where he caught each insect. *Next to the Flint River, Bainbridge Landing; Mosquito Creek Bridge; Boat house, Lake Seminole.* Looking at his face as he

37

murmurs the names of places, I imagine he hears a humming, feels the damp heat of the hot yellow summer, sees the cool green of leaves.

Eventually he decides he has to have the leaves, too, and begins walking in the woods collecting plants: ferns, flowers, weeds, even plants that grow under water in Lake Seminole. These he dries and presses between rough pieces of paper right beneath their Latin names.

One summer morning, my father takes me and my brothers and sister along on one of these walks through the woods at Faceville Landing. We pass a waterfall and he notices a tiny plant, its leaves a variegated green. This, I've never seen before, he says, stopping to bend over the plant. He plucks it from the earth. Something about that, my father plucking the tiny plant from the soil, made me think of him as an Adam. After all, he discovered the plant, I thought; no one had ever seen it before. But it had a name, *Trillium*, and once we saw the first one, we saw another and another and another. Every time I saw one, though, I'd think–there's that plant my father discovered.

But my father wasn't an Adam. He was a child like my brothers and sister and me–he was as astonished at the natural world as we were, or maybe we were astonished at the natural world because of him. When my sister and I were knobby-kneed, flat-chested little girls, my father took us for rides in the back of his government truck as he cruised down the river road. The air was cool, fragrant with the delicate scent of pink mimosas. We lay flat on the cold metal bed of the truck, looking at sky, clouds, trees, the world above our town. We played a game of guessing where we were by looking at the lacy branches of trees. We could always guess our grandmother's street because oaks dripping with Spanish moss grew together over the road like giant hands laced together, blocking out the sky. My father drove us all over town as light faded and we looked at the world of tree branches and clouds hovering right over our heads, changing right before our eyes, a world we never really noticed when we were upright.

Years later, my father arranged with the government pilot to take me up in a little Cessna. We flew into the same blue sky that hovered over my sister and me on our truck rides, then sailed out over a shimmering Lake Seminole then back over town, the airplane buzzing like a giant bumblebee. From my perspective Chattahoochee looked insubstantial, the buildings blocky and small like a play town. I put my hand out, covered the whole thing from one end to the other. I knew I didn't belong on those narrow streets, couldn't make myself fit between the lines, and I knew it was OK. My brothers and sister and I were the only kids in the neighborhood who knew what an *Aedes Aegypti* was. We were the only kids in the neighborhood who let mosquitoes bite us while we looked closely at the markings on their legs and wings, trying to decide to what species they belonged.

Just as I learned there were hundreds of types of mosquitoes, I learned there were fathers and then there were fathers: Sonny Burton, handsome and clean cut; Bobby Holt, hyper masculine, mean as a pit bull; Henry York, chief cop, benign and wise like Andy of Mayberry. These men fit into the parameters of the popular conception of manhood: good looks, a willingness to fight, a sense of authority. Then there were the fathers who beat their children, fathers who drank, who ran around on their wives. One father even cruised the public restrooms looking for men.

Unlike any of those men, my father wasn't stand-up handsome or a fighter or an authority figure or an outlaw. He belonged to the species of men raised by women. Of course all men come from women, but my father had been surrounded by female flesh his whole life. He never knew his own father, who had shot himself in the head when Daddy was only six months old. He had one brother and three older sisters. His mother was a red-headed fireball, a judge in Coffee County, Georgia. She fathered Daddy as best as she could–even giving him a job as her clerk–and he in turn mothered us, peeling potatoes for dinner, shucking corn, snapping beans, churning ice cream, washing our clothes, whipping our asses, carrying us in his arms. My sister called him *Mama*.

Daddy was also shaped by my mother, a dreamer stuck in a less than ideal reality–raising four children in a small Florida town known for its mental institution. My mother was clinically miserable in fits and starts and we rode her moods the way you ride in a car that sputters and jerks along. We could've gotten out and walked, but . . .

I often wondered why my father stuck by her, but I know it was because she was beautiful and passionate and she could be charming when she wanted to be. That combination–of being raised in a family of women and living with my mother–convinced my father that women ruled the world. Especially unpredictable ones.

In fact, I probably have my mother to thank for the close relationship I developed with my father. Some days I was so overwhelmed by the anxiety of living with her, that I couldn't make it all the way to school, even though it was only a block from our house. One morning I walked along behind my brothers, lugging my red plaid book satchel, trying to be excited, but a feeling of dread kept rippling through my stomach. Then all of a sudden it was like a big torrent of water gushed out of nowhere and knocked me over, the water carrying me back down the hill toward our house. I ran as fast as I could, back to the house, back to Mama, my feet pounding the ground so hard my knees hurt. I ran up to the big sliding glass door on the back of our house and pressed my face to the cold glass, banging and crying till my knuckles bruised.

Mama didn't take my panic very seriously. She finished what she'd been doing, then casually slid the door open and let me fall into the room. Then she called Daddy home from work to come and take me to school.

First he drove me uptown to the dime store. The door opened with a jingle of bells. He guided me to the toy section, walking across the creaking floors past Mrs. Bevis with her black cat-eye glasses and her rows of Sugar Babies and Black Crows. He didn't say a word. I picked up a blue wooden yo-yo and he paid for it, then scooped me up in his arms and carried me to the car. He drove me to school, then we walked together down the halls, the smell of varnish heavy in the air. I wouldn't let him leave. He sat in a tiny wood chair across the table from me in Mrs. Ball's first grade class, cutting flowers out of red and yellow construction paper with nubby little scissors, until Mrs. Ball whispered in his ear and he left without me even noticing.

I didn't notice a lot of things my father did for me until after he was gone. He died when I was twenty-one years old. But in that short time he managed to put some ideas into my head, to shape the way I viewed the world. And he did it without even seeming to try. He set up spelling contests between my brothers and me. Once I got a nickel for spelling *tiger*. I still remember how superior I felt to my brothers, how important the word *tiger* seemed—spelling it was like conjuring the wild animal itself. My father encouraged me to show off with words. At the supper table, while plunking an ear of corn onto my plate, he would ask me to spell words like *lackadaisical* or *photokinesis*. I went on to become a champion. I could spell words I'd never heard before, could figure out their meanings from the Latin roots. I felt possessed as letters lined themselves up inside my head. Letters led to words and words led to sentences, and by the time I was five I was reading all by myself.

When I started school, and once I got over my fear of actually making it up the street to sit in the first grade class, my teacher would take me upstairs to humiliate the fourth graders, making me read their history book to them. I decided I wanted to be a writer. Not because I'd read volumes of Shakespeare, but because words felt natural to me, like air. I never struggled with them. Teachers complimented me; the local paper published an essay I wrote about a fishing trip I took with the Boy Scouts. My father thought I should be a journalist. He didn't mention typing.

1977

One Saturday morning when I was 18 or 19 years old, living on my own in Tallahassee, Florida, I was lying in bed asleep, my girlfriend twined around me, when I felt someone looking at me. I woke up and there, in the crack of the bedroom door, was my father's face, hanging in space. He had come to take me grocery shopping, something he did once a week. His face disappeared, and I got up, got dressed and walked out into the dining room and hid behind a newspaper as I drank coffee. He didn't say a word about what he'd just seen. He took me out and we bought groceries, and then he took me to lunch. We never discussed that moment, which must have been a moment of discovery for him. But the women in his life had prepared him for the idea that women do what women do. His mother had prepared him for Mama. As a county judge, she came into contact with all sorts of people and she told Daddy that she expected people not to behave the way most people thought they would. And Mama had prepared my father for me, for the idea that anything could happen at anytime. She'd already figured me out.

Daddy must've taken those lessons to heart. Later that year, when my girlfriend broke up with me and ran off to Mississippi, I was devastated. Somehow I talked her into a reconciliation. My father offered to drive me out to see her. On the way, maybe just as we hit Mobile, Alabama, he gave me the only piece of advice on love I ever got from him. *It doesn't matter who you fall in love with, just make sure they are intelligent.*

1998

I have lived nearly half my life without my father, but he has managed to stay with me. I felt his presence early on when I struggled to type my stories, wondering what he would think of my writing, wondering if he knew I was a writer.

I am a parent, too, and on those days when I am my most

pliable and most genial; when I say to my oldest son, *OK, OK, I'll drive you to St. Marks to see the dead alligator,* I feel like my father must have felt–four kids begging him for popsicles, or rides in the country, begging him for something: Daddy, do this, do that, and he, always, like a gentle bear, doing his best to comply. When I am standing on the edge of that brackish pool of water, my oldest son measuring the gator off by walking next to him, wondering aloud what caused his death, my youngest squirming in my arms, screwing his face up at the smell, but unable to take his eyes off the great dead creature lying beneath the palms, I understand why my father was so compliant. He liked being led by curious children to mysterious places.

I always feel my father's presence out of doors, whether my sons and I are hiking at St. Marks or walking along the Apalachicola River looking for pottery shards. My boys have inherited their grandfather's eye for odd-shaped rocks and funny-looking plants. They drop to their knees in the woods to look more closely at bugs crawling through the grass, and I stand aside, looking at their curved backs through my father's eyes.

These days I take my sons out to the baseball field to bat and play catch. Baseballs smell the same way they did thirty years ago, when my father used to take me and my brothers and sister out to play: red clay, leather, neatsfoot oil. My boys are barefoot on the red clay, and I am my father, pitching slowly, saying the words, *Keep your eyes open; keep your eyes on the ball.*

Duke

Jewelle Gomez

My father had two wives simultaneously when I was growing up, neither one my mother: Henrietta (my favorite) and Tessie. They lived in harmony and actual support of each other at opposite ends of our hometown, Boston. Objectively, that's the most remarkable thing about Duke. But the list of things I know from him, about myself and the world, weaves around me like the shawls that grandmothers are supposed to make. I feel the nappy wool of his self very close to me: the sensibilities of a charming Black bartender, relatively invisible in an economically depressed city in the 1950s and '60s, in a neighborhood trembling on the edge of something called urban renewal, or later called gentrification. We came to think of it simply as urban removal.

Each weekend I visited him at either one of his two households, trying to slip in between the stepsisters and brothers, stepcousins and stepaunts, as if I'd been there all the time and was not a weekend guest. I did chores. I went to bed when I was told. But it was always clear I was there for him. We strode through the South End as a team, so clearly cut from the same cloth it hardly mattered if we spoke at all. And the charm and style for which he was known was transferred to me almost by default. It was like being the stars of a rhythm and blues song. *Duke, Duke, Duke, Duke of Earl.*

He was what they used to call "heavyset, but neat." My stepsisters called him Jackie Gleason because he had the same build, wore exquisitely cut clothes, and was nimble and witty. It was magical to me that my father was the bronze doppelganger for a famous star. Coupling that with his being well-known and well-liked on the block made him a celebrity to me.

The different thoughts that come to mind to create the picture of who he was are colorful and varied. The clothes, of course. Mohair sweaters, Italian knits, sharkskin slacks with knife-sharp creases, perfectly tailored camel hair coat, worn just the way the Black men do. My favorite look was crisp Bermuda shorts, black knee socks, and loafers or deck shoes. The tempting mocha of his knee showing between the socks and shorts as he glided down West Newton Street turned the heads of most women, and many men. Maybe I liked that outfit because it was one I could emulate. Sometimes he'd let me wear his shorts and shirts or sweaters. Oversized clothes were in, and we'd go walking in the neighborhood on errands or for a drive to get his car washed. Duke and Little Duke, as we were called by the patrons in the Venice Tavern, the 411 Lounge, and the Regent.

He took me on my first trip to an airport. He took me to my first teenage music concert–Jackie Wilson–because he got free tickets for helping the promoter with security. I never could identify the exact nature of his help, though, since he was hardly a muscle man. He even cried if my stepcousins got spankings. When I went to the store to buy his cigarettes I'd repeat the name of his brand, "Herbert Taretons," over and over until it because an unrecognizable mantra. But Freddie, in Braddock's Drugstore, knew me.

I was allowed to stay up until Duke got in from work. Boston's blue laws usually brought him home by half past midnight. His tip change jangled in his pockets as he loosened the waist on his pants, then held them up delicately with the hand that also held a lit cigarette. The other hand usually clutched a mayonnaise jar full of iced water. He moved elegantly across the room to sit at the kitchen table with contentment written across his face. If he'd had too much to drink, he moved even more elegantly. He was a man happy to have family, and having two of them was only one of the indications.

He, like the women in my family, loved to talk. He'd sit at Henrietta's kitchen table for hours telling stories about bar patrons, commenting on the news in the *Record American*, which he read while eating, watching television, and talking. He would tell jokes with no punch lines, and we'd all laugh until we cried. He laughed until he cried. Turning the pages of the paper, he'd read quietly for a while, then look up at the TV and make a trenchant observation about something that'd just appeared on the screen, like, "That guy (Ross Martin/"The Wild Wild West") has the worst collection of fake mustaches I've seen since Mona Lisa." And Henrietta, Allan, Bonita, Katherine, and any neighbor's kid who might be spending the night and I would fly off in gales of laughter again.

I had weekly tasks, like all the kids, but mine were related to my father's room. I'd spend hours there just being with his things, reading his stacks of magazines–*Gentlemen's Quarterly*, *Negro Digest*, *Ebony*, *Yachting* (he read the last one regularly, though to my knowledge he'd never been on a boat in his life). I read *The Well of Loneliness* and my first James Baldwin books from the unceremonious pile of novels that grew and shrunk and grew beside his desk. I separated his cufflinks, straightened his desk, folded his sweaters, and counted and stacked his tip change into the neat piles from which he'd pay me.

I'd play his records as I dusted and returned them to their sleeves. Then I would devise a better categorizing system as I refiled them in the newest of the many contraptions for record storage he was always bringing home. One Saturday afternoon he asked me who my favorite singers were. I said Billie Holiday and Arthur Prysock. He beamed and said, "I always knew you'd have good taste." I was eleven years old, and in the thirty-odd years since, I've measured all success against the pleasure that his expression of pride gave me.

At some point we made a deal: He'd teach me bartending, and I'd teach him Spanish from my high school text. He really wanted to learn Portuguese; that's what his father's people were. But I'd examined the multilingual pamphlets that the Christian Scientists left everywhere in our neighborhood and I was never able to make sense of them. Our commitment to these lessons didn't last long, however. His schedule was often erratic, and mine became more so as I grew into a teenager. We really didn't mind, though, since the deal had simply been a device to make sure we spent time together. That never changed: I'd always wait up until he got home from work, or when I started going out he'd wait up for me.

He had beautiful hands which I sometimes manicured. I loved the cool softness of his skin and the way his hands looked both masculine and feminine. He usually wore one of three rings–a Masonic ring with one diamond, or a white gold ring with many small diamond chips, or an onyx ring with a small diamond in its center. He advised me to never wear diamonds to a job in front of white people. He said that no matter what they said they'd be jealous and not want to pay you properly. He also warned me that gold cars blow up. Not an outlandish admonition in light of the fact that three gold Cadillacs had done just that to him. He'd departed from his usually rather conservative beige or blue Cadillac one year to purchase the gold one. Its engine exploded. The dealer quickly replaced it with another. Its engine exploded. The dealer immediately replaced that with another. It caught on fire. My father declined a fourth and switched instead to muted pink with assorted customizations thrown in, along with a free tour of the big Cadillac showroom for me.

I saw my father intentionally do something to upset another person only once. Every Saturday morning Christian proselytizers would ring neighborhood doorbells to preach the gospel or sell copies of The Watchtower. Some people welcomed their visits, usually older folks who received little attention from the outside world, or those who'd been anticipating some sort of conversion for years. But at Henrietta's house it was kind of a joke seeing who'd be stuck answering the bell and then have the impossible task of getting rid of them politely. Once I listened (from behind a bedroom door) to my twelve-year-old stepcousin, Allan, trapped for fifteen minutes on the stairwell, unable to maneuver them back out the door. One Saturday we ignored the bell, but my father was half-asleep and annoyed as hell. He went to the front door naked as a bird. The only thing between him and the gospel was the door's glass window panes. It was some time before they called on us again.

When I think of my father, I hear the sound of excited young voices, "Here comes Uncle Duke!" The words would spread through the gang of kids, and we'd be at the door before he could close the front gate. When an adult got desperate disciplining one of us, she'd just say, "I'm gonna have to tell Duke!" All misbehaving ceased. You could almost sense our actual regret at having ever misbehaved at all. I think none of us wanted to risk losing his respect, or disappointing him, or being sent to bed without listening to him tell stories.

My mother, who visited me at my great-grandmother's house where I lived, was beautiful and talented, even glamorous. But she was not one of those ex-wives who was buddies with her ex-husband. She was always cordial to my father, but their relationship was a prickly area we avoided. She had her own family, too, so the two of them remained in distinctly separate domains that rarely intersected–only for my Holy Communion, my high school graduation, or looking at old family photos. But my mother's mother and my great-grandmother thought like I did: my father was magic.

He seemed to know things that others didn't, or accept new information so easily it felt as if he already knew it to be true. He and Henrietta were, for example, the only adults to like my hair when I got an Afro in 1968. Once, when I was very young, maybe six or seven, he bought us each a pint of strawberries while we were visiting his mother. She looked horrified when she realized we were getting down to the last berry and said, trying not to sound hysterical, "Now, John, you know that girl's allergic!" He looked up at her as if he, too, were seven and said, "But, Mother, we wanted them." In spite of my previous allergic reactions, I never broke out in a rash or got sick that time. It's not a bad thing for a kid to think her parents are magic.

When I was in college he told Henrietta to talk to me about birth control. She was embarrassed; I was mortified. It was a smart thing for him to have done because while living with my great-grandmother provided an extraordinary perspective on life, sex education was not part of it. He was only a bit late.

Only once did he interfere in my social life. Not with the Bynums' boy, snobby son of local West Indian politicians, or Dennis, the gambler, but with George, whom I'd met through friends and who lived in New Jersey. I was seventeen, he'd gotten through his Viet Nam tour, and in my crowd that made him irresistible. One Friday my father stopped to talk to me before he went to work at the bar. He said George would be giving me a call but wouldn't be visiting again. I was stunned, but I knew there had to be a reason. He said George drank too much and didn't really have anything to offer me; that he'd talked with George by telephone in New Jersey and they'd agreed I should finish high school before I have dates with a boy from out of town. And he said I was smarter than George. I hadn't realized that last part until he pointed it out. I thought about it quite a bit and was fascinated that someone else, my father especially, could make a judgment that I was smart, that I might even be smarter than another person.

You usually think your parents will live forever. Your world couldn't exist without them. When Duke got cancer, I figured he was still magic, what's to worry. During the last years of his illness, when I was in college, I visited him regularly after class and on the weekends, as usual. The stepkids always left us some time alone, although they still hung out as long as they could listening to him tell stories. Being bedridden hadn't stopped his mouth. Once when I was with him he said rather abruptly, "You know Allan's a faggot?" There was no special inflection. He might just as easily have said, "You know your cousin is a Democrat?" It was much like when my grandmother had used the word *bulldagger*: words from their world not meant to harm but to describe. Of course I knew. I thought of Duke's friends from the bar–Maurice, Miss Kay–drag queens that he regularly served at the bar and in his home. I wasn't sure what he was saying.

"I wanted somebody else to know besides me."

I like that he kept watching out for our futures, even then. I wish that I'd told him I was a dyke and everything was alright, that Allan wasn't in it alone.

Having two wives at the same time did seem unusual to me when I was a kid, but it never seemed unnatural in my father. As I grew older and examined it from all sides, I applied the socioeconomic realities, the polygamous theories of Afrocentric culture, the philandering male archetype. I decided none of these applied to Duke. Essentially he liked women, liked talking to them and spending time with them. Something else we had in common. Actually, he liked people. That's why he surrounded himself with them and talked about them all the time. Maybe that was his magic.

He slipped into a coma while watching the Red Sox on TV—not uncommon in Boston (that would have been a Duke joke). Henrietta and I sat with him until the game was over. I hated to let him go.

My Father

Janice Gould

I have tried to understand
what makes me afraid, wondering
what my sisters and I will do
with the body of my father
when he dies.
While in his seventies
he changed his sex,
becoming a woman
like us.

As a man, my father was not beautiful.
The skin on his chest was fish white,
he was ruddy at the neck,
his muscles were stringy.
The veins showed on the backs of his hands.
Standing, he gave no pose of strength,
nothing stern, nothing possessive.
He never wished to take up space.
Of the two, my mother was the angrier:
her curses brought my father to shame.
I remember his response to her,
the set line of his mouth,
his lips pressed firmly together.

As a woman, is my father beautiful?
Sometimes in the morning
he calls me long distance.
His voice is softer.
I know it's the voice he uses as Cynthia.

He asks how I am.
I want to say, "I am trying
to deal with my fear of you.
If it weren't for that,
I'd be fine."

In the letters he wrote me
after my mother died,
he said, "When you last came home,
I'm sure you noticed
I've changed. I have been taking hormones
these last few years.
It must be no surprise."

He wrote, "Now that I am a woman
I like to go dancing.
One night Eduardo walked me to my car.
As we stood there, Eduardo wanted to hug me.
I allowed him to put his arms around me.
Suddenly he was feeling me up,
his hands on my breasts.
It was a strange sensation.
I liked it very much.
I don't know if I want to see him again."

Those letters!
I threw them on the floor.
I wanted to stomp on them.
"Your mother," he wrote,
"got the notion when you were young
that you were not normal.
Perhaps it was because
you hated to wear dresses.
She took you to the pediatrician one day,
remarking that if he found anything wrong with you
she would kill you,

then kill herself. Of course,
after the doctor poked and prodded,
he declared there was absolutely
nothing wrong with you."

"Your mother," he wrote again,
"was no saint. Your cousin Elaine
was not your cousin at all
but a half sister by an Indian father,
your mother's lover.
I agreed to raise her as my daughter,
but your mother was so hard on the poor girl
she ran away. Your mother would never
acknowledge her as her own."

"Don't tell your sisters any of this,"
he begged. "It must remain a secret."

O, my father,
father I never knew,
father who never was
yet was my only father,
who do you imagine I am?

Would my father remember the time
I tried to run away from home?
Up as early as him,
my suitcase already packed
and placed on the dark front porch,
I caught the first bus downtown.
He never even knew that I left.
Later he found me at the Greyhound station,
bus ticket in hand.
"Let's go home," he said.
"She hates me," I said.
"I know," he replied.

Then I wept.
I wanted him to hug me,
but he stood, embarrassed,
his arms at his sides.
"Please," he whispered,
"don't make a scene in public."

What will my sisters and I do
on the day of your death?
Where will you be?
At home,
or in the apartment you rented
in that city we do not know?
Will someone be with you?
You have always been so alone.
Will your death come in the fall
or the spring?
Will it be when the hills
have turned green in California?
Will the pear orchards be in blossom?
Will you die on the interstate
near a fallow field
where blackbirds have settled
because it is evening?

But I don't want to think about it.
Whom will we tell?
What will we tell them?

"No one will be able to tell the difference,"
my father wrote. "I will be anatomically perfect."

What Died with Him

Holly K. Iglesias

He was everything good about October.
   Ripe persimmons.
   Hard pears.
   His birthday.
   Candy loot.
   Leaves underfoot.
   An old jacket.
   Low-riding moon.
   Wedding days: my parents, grandparents, brothers.
   Milkweed eruption.
   Bough of bittersweet.

I come to speak of the dead who love me. Like a motherless child, I'm a long way from home, a long way from my home. Home in his heart. They say we learn to babble in mother's belly; that our grief on the outside translates to nonsense, a thick gurgle that no one wants to hear. I come to speak of those who loved me, the dear ones, dead. I sat with my father as he died; watched him die, attentive to the flutter of his eyelids, the race of breath. A vigil for the rise of panic, ready to palm it back into his chest. I told him to keep his eyes on me–*Watch me, Dad. Slowly, in and out. Slowly yes out ah*–as I watched his rush to be gone, the shock of confinement, straining against the straps. Drooling a rant, then a coo, oatmeal on the blanket, whose bed? teeth in a glass, tubes, tubes, charts clamped to the railing. Confused and weeping, he swore he didn't want to break my heart. I come now to speak; this hallowed ground. I had nothing to ask of him at the end. All had been given; there was nothing to ask.

* * *

He went well before dawn on a December morning, the sky still full of night and the bitter bite of cold. A full moon, and stars crackling through imponderable distance. By himself, in a steel-frame bed, sheets reeking of industrial bleach.

Against his wishes. I come to speak. His nightmare, *staring at me*. His desire clear, in writing: no wake, no gawkers. Not like his mother, who loved a crowd, loved a crowd to love her. Not like my mother who knows *what's right, a proper burial, only right*. She has always had her way with him and this will be no different. My sister and I watch the line move past him, the line staring at him and the pretty box that would have rankled him. No shelter, *don't let them*. To speak of the dead. His mother preceding him by a slim margin, her passing sudden. What sudden? he joked; nothing sudden about a hundred-year-old woman dying. All the same he wasn't prepared for it; year of the great flood, counting survival in inches and feeling the mud move in.

Though separated by generation and heritage, my father and my son shared a disdain for public rites and keen desire to say their piece while there was time. One, newly a man, raw, weeping beside the other's bed, softly pressed the words into his cheek: *I'll miss you, Grandpa*. Both of them bereft, beyond protection.

Cloying heat, the room choked with mourners upholstered in tasteful, dark wool, dabbing mascara with Irish linen hankies. My daughter in a corner, sullen and swollen-eyed, fetal in a velveteen chair; my sister smoothing her hair. We were the other women in his life. Now, three of us survive him; three of us, the bold ones, scarred, defiant, golden. Unlike his sons, who are docile as pages, who are hers. We are unmoored, the room adrift, careening. The anchor he taught us to strain against now loosed and each of us suddenly random as our birth; blood's basin drained. We lean into one another, three, the small clutch of us; cleave unto me!

What died with him.

*   *   *

The door to his den is slatted with shutters. Behind it, his preserve, a retreat, a museum, a hive–typewriter, reel-to-reel tape recorder, a hi-fi I can use if there are absolutely no scratches on my records. Hundreds of books, a bronze bust of Lincoln, white marble mortar and pestle, his 1959 Pharmacist-of-the-Year clock, the lava lamp my mother hates because she doesn't like gizmos or doodads. A brown Morocco case that contains liquor bottles and a Martini shaker; the glass decanter with a music-box base that plays "How Dry I Am" every time Uncle John pours a glass of Bardenheier's Concord grape wine. The couch is modern–no arms, rattan back, cushions covered in a nubby orange plaid. A humidor of cherry tobacco next to the rack of pipes, a Bavarian stein, the ceramic skull full of pennies. On the walls are framed pictures of ancient Greek doctors and Egyptian alchemists, Mom's graduation photo, one of me and my sister in matching dresses, and a charcoal caricature of him during the war. His honorary Cardinal baseball player certificate. In the closet, cartons of magazines and stamp catalogues, his tan yard-work jacket and the wine-red wool smoking robe with tattersall collar and cuffs. The file cabinet brimming: deeds, diplomas, honorary discharge papers; stock certificates and licenses; a folder for each child of report cards, vaccination records, letters to Santa; mailing list of GI buddies, two family trees, love letters. A bank of shelves for photo albums, another for LP's. On his desk, an apothecary jar lamp, a leather-bound blotter, a flat chrome address file with a lid. The shifting miniature treasures in the top drawer: brass brads, gummed labels, scalloped disk of flints, loose leads, Italian coins, a tin of Sen-Sen, his silver ID bracelet, Florentine stiletto, our mother's high school ring–*Saint Joseph's Academy, 1942*. A deep, deep drawer; a place for private messages–*Dad, I'm sorry I forgot*; where he stashed a German POW's Luger and the snapshot of bodies in a heap.

The drugstore in East Saint Louis is forty miles from our house, so far from the manicured suburbs that it seems like another world.

He likes it over there, the deserted stock yards and derelict warehouses; remembers when the place was hopping with the jazz clubs and zoot suits and hip flasks of hooch. Over on the East Side, yes indeed; gonna leave that crewcut grass behind. During summers and vacations, I work with him, stocking shelves with Prell and Ben-Gay, decanting astringents and cough syrup, covering the cash register after Margrethe leaves. The pharmacy occupies a large corner of Grandpa Pidgeon's, an enormous discount store where the hardscrabble farmers and urban blighted of southern Illinois go for cheap merchandise. No frills or hype, strictly a bare-bones volume business. My mother calls it crass, the concrete floors and chintzy goods; but Dad says you can't complain about the college tuition and trips to Europe it pays for. I love this place, and I love working with him; the hum of him behind the prescription counter as he cuts deals with distributors, counts out pills, types labels with two fingers. His high-necked uniform tunic with cloth-knot buttons, his name embroidered in blue across his chest: *Ralph Krummenacher, R.Ph.* The heft of his key ring and the jangle of change in his pocket. In the luncheonette, the waitress who smiles at him, then me: *Chicken-fried steak with onion gravy, slaw and cobbler if we got it–right, Mr. K?* But he barely touches it; always too stoked to eat, smoking instead, talking with me about books as I eat.

Driving home, we cross the river at Eads Bridge–a long string of coal barges below us, steel stumps of the Gateway Arch above the landing, refinery flames fading in the distance–and join the stream of downtown traffic. He doesn't wear a hat; he's Mister Smooth, raising his chin to blow a blue wisp of smoke out the crack in his window. He twirls the dial past news and sports, past Montovani and Mitch Miller, until he finds what he wants: the gravel and honey of Louis Prima and Keely Smith, or the sizzle of a wire brush on a snare drum, or the luscious fog of Ella's voice. He flicks his wrist as he snaps to the beat, head bobbing. Nods at me–*What a sweet sweet life, kiddo*–winking.

*   *   *

I can't know if the place I held in my father's life was a result of the rift between him and my mother. But I feel fairly sure that our closeness was helped by the fact that I presented him with no rivals, or at least no male competitors for my affection. I didn't date in high school. You could say I wasn't interested; you could say I was a nerd or that I was queer. Each one bears a partial truth, but what matters is that I thought I was sexless. I know that this helped to ease tensions between my dad and me when I was a teenager, because he treated my sister, who was most definitely interested in boys, quite differently–with a disconcerting blend of awe and panic.

The two times he blew up at me involved clothes, on the surface. They also stand out among the few times I called him unfair. Once, in eighth grade, I asked permission to buy a new pair of shoes with my babysitting money. Although he OK'd the purchase, when I showed him the shoes–shoes I'd coveted for months in Baker's window, shoes that would change my life, fire-engine red pumps with a princess heel and lots of toe cleavage–he yanked the box from my hand and ordered me to return them the next day. End of discussion.

Then, sometime shortly after that incident, his business partner came to our house early one morning for a meeting. Awakened by their voices, I went downstairs to the den in my nightgown to see who was there. As I was saying good morning, Dad rushed to the door, almost knocking me over. Grabbing me tightly by the arm, he directed me back upstairs, practically hissing in my ear: *Don't you ever expose yourself like that again. You go to your room right now and dress yourself properly before you come downstairs again.*

The last time my brothers treated me like family, we were searching for him, trying to get our hands on him. We gathered in the den, early morning, the arc of time and its tasks–school, work, errands–truncated; fresh from the hospital and its raw lights and paperwork, from the sight of his body being rolled out the service door on a gurney. Father, father.

When his father had died, he was seated in a Knights of Columbus hall, watching me compete in the archdiocesan spelling bee. His partner appeared in the hush of the room, tapping him on the shoulder, which caused him to grab his coat and leave, quickly nodding a dose of confidence to me from the door. I lost in the final round; inattentive to the definition, too eager to be done with it. As I blurted o-r-a-c-l-e, a dear one was dying. His tender father–*could eat him without salt, that darling Rudy*–a man who adored his wife, clung to her; who scolded his first-born for defiance, and loved him for it. Father and son, both druggists, mixing, measuring, counting. The father's swift end, collapsed behind the prescription counter of another man's store, and our fatherless dad, hatless, alone in the morgue to identify the body, nodding: *Yes, that's my father.*

So here was our turn, shortly past sunrise in winter. Huddled in his den, fingering shelves and drawers for some trace of him, inhaling the scents that lingered–pouch tobacco, grease pencils, Army blanket, Old Spice. Oh his raw cheeks after he shaved! that shocking slap and his laugh as we watched the whisker-flecked lather melt in the sink. It failed to register that he was utterly gone, as we pawed through photo albums for evidence, stroking white-ink captions in his unmistakable script, idly licking down loose corners. His was the eye framing every picture, the hand that glued us into these books to keep us familiar with ourselves. There: I found him: our father, a lanky shadow angling across the bottom of a serrate-edged black-and-white, a ramp at my feet, his first-born, learning to walk.

You would never call my mother hysterical. She is a tart sorbet of elegance and composure, not one to squeal or gush or shriek. Imagine, then, how her screaming terrified us.

We were on vacation; a family-vacation-of-the-damned to be more specific. The wife hungry for culture and cuisine, the husband hell-bent on visiting every historic battleground between Chattanooga and New Orleans. Two youngsters who wanted nothing more than a bottle of YooHoo and a cheap souvenir every fifty miles, and a sullen teenager determined to make the misery of all passengers in the station wagon match her own. The wife insistent upon a daily meal at a "real restaurant"; the husband's vocal complaint about the effects on his wallet of one child who wouldn't share a hot dog with her brother even though she couldn't eat a whole one, and another who refused all solid foods except Rice Krispies and Maine lobster. The children who balked at motels with shuffleboard courts but no pool; who giggled and snorted each time the mother slammed an imaginary brake in order to alert the father that his driving was giving her a case of nerves. The eldest requesting a detour to Montgomery to see the Confederate flag flying over the capitol with her own two eyes; badgering her father that his beloved Civil War was no more history than she was.

Suffice to say that when we pulled into a motor court in Port Gibson, Mississippi, at dusk in the summer of 1963 and found accommodations that included swimming pool, snack bar, "real restaurant" and a pair of adjoining rooms, everyone was relieved. Our parents installed us in one room and established the other as their own by setting a leather liquor case on the dresser. We were to fold our clothes neatly and put on our swimsuits; then sit quietly until Dad was ready to take us to the pool. Which we did; until we heard Mom scream.

Because the door between our rooms was locked, and because at least two of us were aficionados of high drama, we used the luggage rack as a battering ram, but to no avail. Then, from the outside, we tried their door on the corridor, which opened–to a vision that no one has since mentioned and probably never will. Our mother, although no longer screaming, whimpered, gasping in spasms for air, and bunched great wads of the tufted bedspread around her like a fabric fort. Dad, wearing her gingham-check bathing suit and pink rubber cap with the seahorse design, at the sight of us executed an odd little prancing step and made Jerry Lewis noises, which we assumed was to assure us that we were in the presence of a riotous gag. He explained that our mother had simply over-reacted due to fatigue and would calm down soon; that he now would go back into the bathroom and put on his swim trunks. Sizing up the situation, I did the only sensible thing. I poured her a glass of scotch; and, while Dad took the little kids to the pool, sat next to her on the corner of the bed, watching *Queen for a Day*.

My sweet-toothed dad, not a candy he wouldn't eat, even though chocolate made him sneeze. Jawbreakers, Necco wafers, sour balls, red hots, jujubes, peanut logs, licorice pipes, horehound drops, Mary Janes, candy canes, marzipan, butterscotch, pecan turtles, divinity, Black Crows, nonpareils, root beer barrels, Tootsie Rolls, atomic fireballs, Turkish taffy.

His savor of words, some rolled around in his mouth like cud, others sucked to transparency or chewed with enormous gusto. He bandied words with us in a game of verbal catch, expecting strong retorts. Highfalutin altekockers, wisenheimer pipsqueak, bellyachers, pooferwillies, fuddy-duddy, schenkel, tickle-locks, perfufnik. A term could suddenly become a name, a joke, and we would find ourselves being introduced to a customer at his store as Applecrombie Perfufnik and her maiden aunt Shleezel. We were adults before we ever suspected that he might have fabricated some of these words. Or admired his invention of a term that served to identify any item he couldn't remember or was too flustered to bother naming: Quick! hand me a schmekel. Where the hell is that schmekel for the barbecue sauce? If you run across any schmekel in that metal drum, just burn it. Wipe that schmekel off your chin.

His rapid-fire questions, to instill us with an appreciation of the order of things, their weight. When was the Battle of Hastings? Bull Run? Who was Art Tatum? Norman Thomas? Alexander von

Humboldt? Where does penicillin come from? How many grains in a dram? What time is it in Rome? Who wrote the Firebird Suite? How much does a gallon of Coke syrup cost? What year was the Saint Louis World's Fair? What's Stan Musial's lifetime batting average?

Wisdom doled out in tidbits: Don't brake on a curve. Just spit it out. If you can't pay for it, don't buy it. You're a lover, not a fighter. Never buy crap. If you lose your nerve, tell a joke. Keep your eye on the ball.

From my father I learned romance; from my mother, remove. Years of observing his adoration of her taught me how to be a lover. My mother, uncomfortable as his beloved to the point of irritation, made being on the receiving end seem highly undesirable. It was years before I found the woman who could show me the pleasure of being lover and loved.

My dad jumped through a lot of hoops to marry my mother. She was the long-awaited daughter of indulgent parents and something of a hot ticket in her crowd. Angular features, hazel eyes, acerbic wit, intelligent, sheltered, high-spirited, stylish. Catholic. He'd given up on his parents' religion before he went into the service and came back from overseas with no interest in going through the motions of any church. Marrying a Catholic girl, the Irish-Catholic girl who was May Queen of Cathedral School, would require a bit more of him than a ring and a solid financial plan for their future. The Church required of him, the prospective, heathen husband, to promise to let his wife raise their children as Catholics, and to restrict their wedding ceremony to the church vestibule, at a far remove from the sacristy. This grated on him; but he was in love, willing to pay the price.

After making my First Holy Communion, I became devout with a fervor known only to eight-year-old girls, awash in the ecstasy of a bride of Christ; eager for the day of my Confirmation when I would join the ranks of His soldiers. Ah, the veil and armor, the delirious metaphorical mix of nuptial and combat. A serious communicant, I confessed weekly and did my penance with a vengeance. Gladly did I take a scouring pad to the filthy oven of my soul so that I, unworthy handmaiden, pitiful supplicant, might receive Him on my knees in a state of purity.

As a suburban child of the mid-century Midwest, my chances for a martyr's crown were slim. Thus I retreated into fantasy, recruiting public school boys willing to play Roman centurion to my Christian slave to tie me to a tree where I could writhe in prayerful agony until my mother called me in for dinner. Although my father was engrossed in *Caesar and Christ* at the time, he had little patience for my more contemporary spiritual struggles. He considered it dangerous, perhaps even cruel, to give *The Lives of the Saints* to a child with a vivid imagination like mine. He warned me that my role-playing would make me soft-headed; that I had bigger fish to fry; that I was giving him the heebie jeebies. He suggested as an alternative turning my energies toward earning a fistful of Girl Scout merit badges, which appealed to my taste for uniforms and soothed the heartbreak of being yet too young for a novice's habit.

Sadly for him, the distraction was short-lived–the nebulous requirements for the "Dabbler" badge frustrating me, our troop leader pregnant–and I turned my attention to his conversion, as was my duty as child of a mixed marriage. Before Monsignor O'Toole explained the intricate pitfalls of such a union, I was enamored of the term; it evoked images of mixed drinks, of highballs and cocktail dresses and smoke-filled nightclubs, the epitome of my parents' relationship beyond the confines of our house. Mixers, slow dancing, double clutch; blenders whirring up exotic concoctions with rum; combustible chemicals spewing green vapor. But O'Toole burst that bubble by informing us that a mixed marriage was almost sure to fail. Even worse, the non-Catholic person, by nature of his unredeemed state, might lure the Catholic away from the bosom of Holy Mother Church. Thus, those unfortunate children among us who were the spawn of such a toxic mixture had our work cut out for us. We were to convert the sinner and bring him into the fold.

This was a dilemma. I loved my father, and his parents, and attending services with them at their Presbyterian church. I admired them for dispensing with kneelers and for singing hymns in English. I even loved the word Protestant; it sounded so rebellious, so exciting, like they always carried torches in one hand and raised a fist for freedom with the other. What was wrong with that? It seemed so American. But my father had disavowed the Presbyterians and all other Protestants for that matter, claiming for himself the status of agnostic, which was beyond the pale. He was a free radical, loose, unclaimed. A real challenge.

So I did what I was taught to do. I forgave him; and told him so. He laughed, which I took as the scorn to be expected, the devil speaking. Standing firm, fingering a rosary in my pocket, I then asked him straight out to convert. He refused, explaining that he had long ago set his sights on Hell because that's where his friends would be, the ones with whom he hoped to spend eternity. This was tougher than I had expected, forcing me to pull out all the stops. I wept; I begged him to do it for my sake. His face reddened; he was furious. He told me that while he admired my efforts to carry out the dictates of my religion that now was as good a time as any to learn the importance of respecting varying points of view. This was the first of many times that he would demand my consideration of a broad spectrum; that he would wax poetic about the infinite shades of gray. He told me that his soul was not my responsibility; and that if I wanted to take up a missionary career I should first devote some time to the study of atrocities committed in the name of Mother Church.

This encounter set the tone for our entire relationship. He held his ground while at the same time taking me seriously. He refused my request without belittling me. Because he argued with me, I knew I was someone to be reckoned with. When we debated, I understood that my ideas and my desires mattered. That I was not to play a game of crocodile tears and pouting petulance.

Although I was unable to draw him into the herd, I felt no sense of defeat or surrender. He had clearly released me from my duty and I was free of conflict, restored to my peculiar position as a child of a mixed marriage. Later, in the new world order of Vatican II, the border disputes between my parents became less fundamental, more stylistic. She Mod and aloof, he in mixed plaids and saddle oxfords, their discord manifesting at the surface.

Lover, mine. Sweet forest canopy, oh mossy floor. Be brook to me, and clearing. Solid floor, my sturdy roof; true like timber, your quiet grain. Hearth, and thrill of flight. Your years on the trail; our two meanders. Well-met, worn and ready, we come home.

She watched me in the throes of his passing. The exhaustion of pleading his case, for the solace of his bed at home; doing battle with my mother and brothers over the place where he would end his days–whose hovering face, whose blanket, which odors the last whiff of time. Fear in the face of his resignation; knowing what he would take with him.

She held me as I tried to cling to him. And again as I let him go.

Would he love her as I do; because I do? I have to trust that he would not turn against me, us. Surely he would love my love of her; surely he loves me still.

And his mother, surely, too, would love me still, her first grandchild, the girl she'd waited for. Say these dead ones love me in my love of her; delight in the savor of our sweetness.

The ones who abide, surely they would not spit me out like sour milk; rush to rinse their mouths of the taste of me. Would wail at the craven hearts, the clamped teeth and hooded eyes; the shame of turning out one of their own. Mother, brothers, the callus of their contempt for my flesh, my love.

At the funeral, I picture him pruning, swabbing an elm with creosote. I am struggling to hold on to the man who relished deep taproots and canopy shade and the solidity of trunks. Who, when love turned against him, built a wall from broken limbs and fallen branches. Broke them down into twigs and jammed them into an eroded berm, banking against the rains that were bound to come. That witless wall became his project, his life's work. He spent himself on it, a place to hide his heart.

Around the time my marriage crumbled, he was finished with the wall. Some said he was mad, but he was saner than the sun and he saved me. He was a broken man, surely; and ill, newly confined to a grueling regimen of dialysis. I was a thousand miles away, and not one to ask. But I too had seen the end of love, could feel myself slipping like mud, and needed his presence. I asked him, *Come, sit in my house; be a rock*; and without hesitation, he did.

Eighteen years prior, I had informed my parents over the telephone, long distance from Miami, that I was getting married the next day to a young Cuban man they'd never met. That he would return the following weekend to Spain, where he was studying medicine and evading the draft, and where I would join him after I collected my things in New Orleans.

Thus began my own mixed marriage. He, an exile, volatile, driven, flamboyant, shrewd, magnetic, the only child of an indulgent mother and a cruel father. I, Midwestern, hungry for experience, flattered by any proposal, facile with languages, at once cynical and Pollyanna-ish, the oldest child of a practical father and an elegant mother. Clueless that my father had set me up to adore a hot-house narcissus. I was young and eager to eat up the world, roam with a brood of my own. Only vaguely aware that I would need to teach my children what I had learned: how to navigate a difficult confluence.

Through some good fortune, I was released, like a gamefish unworthy of the sport. Pitched into a current that swept me back to myself, to an unanswered hunger, to the woman who loves me. Still.

My imagination insists that my mother married my father because he was an oddball, which amused her; irreverent, and thus titillating; a romantic who was crazy about her, which she had come to expect. That over time these qualities lost their sheen; bored her, failed to please. And that she wanted to be free of him.

I am sure that he found her self-absorption attractive, that sense of entitlement almost regal. For I, too, have been awestruck by such magnificent composure, drawn by her cool reserve; thrilled to the privilege of her affections. Because the end is always in the beginning, his story ends in sorrow, awaiting death aware that she was counting the days, that I was watching them unravel. I tell myself he could not have known that the one he adored could turn. *Could cut the cord   could spit us out   oh cleave*

Teeth ground down to snarling stumps, a banshee howls for woe of the years laid waste. So sing to me now of the ones who endure, of a burning heart and my path to you, mavourneen. Ah, speak to the woman who loves you, my winking lovely, of the ones who love us still among the living.

Tzimtzum

Helena Lipstadt

There is a concept in Judaism called *Tzimtzum*. It addresses the problem: If God is everywhere, how is there room for anything else in the universe? The answer is: God consciously contracted, pulled back, made room for something else to appear, to exist. In this contraction there is a flavor of delight in the creation and of self sacrifice.

* * *

The first time I take LSD, I see the laundry line of white sheets stretched across my windows turn into a line of huge white tulips slowly undulating. I look down and see my lover Peter's face transmogrify into the face of my father. In the space of one second each, my father's face and Peter's face replace each other under me. I keep moving, pushing down my dread, keep building my passion, watch the faces change, Peter, David.

Afterwards, I take out the image, choke my father's face *get out of here* twelve years old again. I slam the bathroom door.

At the kitchen table, across the daily paper, my father stretches out his hand toward my mother. He looks at her, his eyebrows raised. She blushes and withdraws. Her eyes are cast down.

I am transfixed by the look in his eyes, her blush, her half smile that lingers. I absorb his reaching hand, lower my lids over my eyes.

* * *

The prom, Dave brings me home pink satin breasts strain into his hand, mouths everywhere the couch creak of steps in the hall

69

my father stands in the doorway   I rocket back from galaxies   *get out of here*   crash in shame.

*   *   *

Early morning in my childhood, he walks in his underwear from his bedroom past my open door to the bathroom. His hand hides his crotch. Curious and repelled I turn away. Why do I turn? He is hiding himself. I turn away and feel ashamed. I shouldn't see what he is hiding. I shouldn't feel curious. Or repelled. I withdraw, suck up his hiding, feel it for him. I make myself–my whole body/mind/spirit/self–small. Or I blow up. Compressed like gunpowder in a chamber, I explode.

*   *   *

I want to unlearn him. By now my withdrawal is automatic. I am split into layers   live in one at a time. Withdraw, explode, withdraw, explode.

*   *   *

Driving in the car he and I sing together, his songs. I know all the words, supply the ones he forgets. I anticipate every pause, his rhythm is my pulse.

*   *   *

The obvious storm in my body. This blossoming, womanizing body. These dangerous breasts, opening thighs. The perfume and heat of my young body filling the space in our house. My hairbrush in the steamy bathroom, my pink lipstick, caterpillar black mascara, spiking each lash wide around my curious eye. My hair curling to my shoulders, my skirt touching the top of my knees. Ironing my clothes in my white nylon slip at the board in the kitchen, I sing with the radio. The fabric is first hot then smooth. I put on the cotton blouse still warm, smooth it over my breasts, my hungry breasts.

*   *   *

I feel my father move back from this fecund wave, move back out of its way horror and confusion of the curving billowing female space of his daughter emitting the smell of sex. I don't want him to withdraw, to lose him, I want him to let me change into a woman, tell me he approves of my beauty and my heat, but he pulls back in horror and confusion. I don't know what or who he sees when he looks at me. I don't want him to leave because I am changing. He keeps pulling back. I bring my lipstick and mirror into my bedroom, shower when he is out of the house, lace my suede boots up to my knee, wear my hair in a French twist, the wildness restrained. Approve of me as I change, the soft baby, the learning girl, the blossom woman, sex rising up like night jasmine. I wash my armpits and starch my blouses, cover the jasmine heat, try to win back the baby-approval. Adopt, absorb his horror and confusion and make it mine, attempt to carry it for him. Save him from it. My job from the first tooth to protect him from harm, from me. He leaves me anyway and I am left carrying his confusion and horror. Braid and twist and iron and still perfume the room with the unbridled smell of me.

*   *   *

It is literally true: I am made from his cells. And I, with no microscope or lab test, recognize these tiny particles, go unerring to a woman who I find out in our years together, can be counted on to carry a clean cotton handkerchief, just like him; who likes to fix the leaking toilet when we're already late leaving the house, just like him; complains when the bills come in, just like him; who draws out my feelings, then criticizes me for them. How I instantly recognize him in her and feel at home: Oh, this is the one, she feels like home, like him. I yearn to have her draw me close in the middle of the day, have her smooth the hair back from my face.

Shooting the Moon

Sheila Ortiz Taylor

Picture me at six streaking through the house and leaping off a short flight of stairs, clad in pajamas with an overlay of underpants and a baby blanket pinned around my neck. Superman, in case the image fails you; I was Superman. I could fly.

Every night I would dream of flight, see myself circling over the local market, waving to the butcher, the produce man, the neighbors, all of whom would look up with wonder and admiration at the flying girl. Each night the dream would include a certain specific clue for achieving flight. It might involve holding my breath, or bending my legs back against my body, or stretching out my hands in a certain aerodynamic fashion at just the right minute. The next morning would find me in my home-fashioned Superman outfit, legs pumping across the patio I used as runway, hurtling myself off the side of a steep hill in the heart of Los Angeles. Then I would pick myself up, examine my knees and elbows for new contusions, and join my family at the breakfast table.

This conviction about unassisted flight certainly guided me safely through one divorce, a dozen or so disastrous love relationships, the Ph.D. program at UCLA, and the successful rearing of two strong and independent daughters. It led to my becoming a writer and an out lesbian at a major university and in a rural community in the South. It prompted me to descend a mall escalator at the age of fifty-one and fling myself into the arms of the woman I had fallen in love with a dozen years before and to marry her in the Unitarian Church before god and everyone.

How did the flying girl metamorphose into the lesbian grandmother? By somehow positioning herself between her practical mother and her dreaming father, then adding a little something all her own.

72

Historically there was, on my mother's side, the privileging of The Mother, particularly in the form of my mother's own mother-worship, a dedication I recognized in all my aunts and uncles, all twelve of them. At the center of life was The Mother, whose continuing presence made them all safe and significant. The corporeal manifestation of the Divine Mother was Della Cabares y Ortiz Shrode, my grandmother, a stocky, brown Mexican-American woman with small hands and fierce determination.

As a child I spent equal time at my mother's house on a hill in Silver Lake and at my grandmother's house in a barrio next to the Los Angeles River. Both houses, one big, one small, were galleries of folk art dedicated to the goddess. Likenesses of the Mother were on every wall, and both houses had small altar niches in which dwelt plaster Virgins in blue *rebosos*, their sheltering arms out-stretched to the troubled or the guilty. My sister and I were usually one or the other, often both.

My father, who preferred to think he had no religion at all, never contradicted or discredited this matriarchal religion. At his core, he, too, was probably a believer. After surviving the courtship of my mother under the rigorous scrutiny of her seven brothers, he took his place with them at the kitchen sink, tossing back shots of tequila. But like all the males in the family, including my grandfa-ther, he clearly accepted that the female principle ruled this house.

The balance of power on the hill was more problematic. Like many Anglo men who marry Latinas, my father wanted to worship without obeying. And probably even worship seemed more inviting and rewarding before marriage than afterward. Daily life tends to wear away the symbolic quality of people, eventually exposing them as the same raw bundle of idiosyncrasies, urges and compulsions as we ourselves are. While the plaster Virgin is likely to stay in her niche, all others in time will climb down and want to direct the course of domestic life.

Bear in mind that my mother was an Aries. Bear in mind she was beautiful and had never lived more than seven miles from Hollywood in her entire life.

In fact, it was partly this beauty which led to the problematic marriage on the hill. My father, hopelessly in love with the enchanting Juanita, whom he had met at the Polar Palace ice skating rink one Saturday afternoon, found himself in the embarrassing position of already being in possession of a wife. I was in my forties when my mother mentioned in an off-hand way the fact of this other wife, this Anglo named Doreen. "I thought you knew," she said, lifting an ironic eyebrow.

So in time my father divested himself of Doreen, courted the mysterious Virgin, and built her a Mexican house on several lots from which one could–by standing on a chair in the dining room–catch a glimpse of the glimmering concrete-enclosed Silver Lake Reservoir several miles away. The house was expensive, a little remote for the fifties, and unlike any other in the neighborhood. It was a dream house, designed by my father himself. It had a maid's room with bath (though never a maid), a game room separate from the house itself (for his poker parties), a music room where he could practice his saxophone and oboe, and a lavish master bathroom with adjoining dressing room for the cosmetic devotions of his beautiful bride. The only thing this house lacked was a bedroom for children.

Obviously my father's dream was to have a lifelong romantic and solitary relationship with the dark exotic woman, while the dark exotic woman's dream was to bear daughters. My mother never entertained the possibility of bearing sons. No, she was going to bear only daughters.

Her other dream was to open her own dressmaker's shop, but this dream conflicted with my father's dream of sequestering the dark woman on a mountain top. No wife of his was ever going to work.

A compromise was struck; daughters were born. We slept in the music room at first, later in the maid's room. But my father's master dream had been compromised in a deadly fashion. He had to share his dark bride with two creatures scarcely more evolved than hamsters.

For several years we seldom saw our father, who worked two jobs, law by day and music by night. He was a faithful and even inspired provider. But I suspect he was also avoiding the hamsters, who by virtue of the carefully worked-out compromise were bathed, fed and put to bed before he got home.

A major change occurred when, by some obscure procedure never revealed to me, we were eventually judged ready to appear at the family dining table with both parents, rather than simply our mother, who customarily smoked and visited with my sister and me while we sat in our pajamas and ate our child dinners. But the change necessitated lessons. Lessons in manners. Napkins belonged in laps, meat must be chewed 100 times, dishes must be passed, conversation supported in both Spanish and English, and milk both poured and consumed without spilling.

In my memory my sister and I knocked over our milk every night for five years. We knew ahead of time we would knock the glass over, just as we knew that the sound of the glass striking the polished surface of the table would drive our father's mind back to those lost intimate dinners with the dark maiden that had taken place by music and candlelight, while his daughters lay in their beds, reading comic books and playing on their quilts with toy soldiers.

But his determination to educate his daughters never faltered from the moment he admitted us to his table. He took us to the public library every two weeks; coached us in rudimentary Spanish; taught us to tie a sheep shank, a bowline and a standing clove hitch; encouraged us to name clouds, to recognize constellations, and to play "The Sheik of Araby" on the tenor saxophone. He drove us to horseback riding lessons and swimming lessons. He tutored us in home maintenance: how to unclog a septic tank; how to prune fruit trees; how to change light bulbs; how to sand, paint, wax, replace, preserve. We knew from him that life was about sustaining what you had and about learning what you didn't know and that these were lifelong activities. He always assumed we would go to college and never assumed–unlike our mother–that we would eventually marry. Everyday life with my father was an intensive training program, an apprenticeship, a stint in boot camp.

My mother pleaded with him to "let us alone." Her own approach to learning was more organic and even wary. Like her brothers and sisters, she mistrusted education, both formal and informal. Intelligence was native, natural, practical. For us she represented the unsystematic, the unpredictable, the intuitive-qualities my father would tend to ridicule and use as a focus for unkind, intellectual attacks that grew, probably, out of his own loss of power and the loneliness he must have felt as the only male in a household where even the parakeet was female.

In retrospect, it seems to me my sister and I were the game board over which our parents struggled and maneuvered. Their attempts to recruit us to one side or the other ironically tended to plunge us into a close and supportive relationship with each other. After we moved into the maid's room at the elevated opposite end of the house, we often felt as alone and unsupervised as the Brontë children. Or, like Christopher Robin, we seemed to have no parents at all. We read, listened to the radio and dreamed. In the rich and companionable solitude of this remote room, my sister went into training as a visual artist and I as a writer.

At regular intervals, we would nevertheless be summoned down from the maid's room to take sides. One night at dinner, my father declared my mother's home-made biscuits hard as hockey pucks. Neither my sister nor I knew what a hockey puck was, but at his invitation we packed up the offending biscuits and carried them outside, where the three of us threw them at the high-tension tower that symbolically enough overshadowed our house, trying to make the night ring with the sound of her domestic failure. That night my sister and I were quiet in the maid's room, contemplative, aware somehow that we had been fooled into betraying our own mother, and somehow ourselves.

Another time, when I came home from school, my mother looked up from her ironing board and gave me an exact total of the shirts, blouses and dresses she had ironed that day, as if her labor were an unreasonable debt I must somehow repay. I will never forget her eyes. Both accusation and warning flared obliquely from their depths. One day I would take my place at the ironing board, they correctly prophesied.

In my own mind, this struggle over allegiances climaxed when my father bought a boat, some time around 1948. His long-standing dream was to sail around the world, but characteristically enough this vision was alien to my mother, whose dream was to own a mink coat. Without consulting her, he came home from work one night to say he had bought a 37-foot unfinished hull of a sailboat. Though my mother never came to share his zeal for sailing, her sense of women's role meant she helped with the finishing work, then crewed and entertained on board for the next five or six years. The master plan called for my sister and me to grow into responsible crew members, whereupon the cruise around the world would begin.

In the meantime, we sailed back and forth from the mainland to Catalina, growing brown and strong, gradually overcoming our inclination toward seasickness and complaint. On one such voyage we moored in Avalon Bay, and after dinner, after the sun was piped down by a Scot on the next boat, we gathered around the dining table for a game of Hearts.

The game embodied a familial ritual. My father would fill the kerosene lamps with fuel, my mother would wipe down the dinette's table top, my sister and I would get out the Bicycle playing cards, and we would all arrange ourselves around the formica table. Custom required my mother to say, "Now how do you play this game?" thus confirming my father's conviction that my mother was basically stupid and that as a young man he had been foolishly beguiled into choosing beauty over wisdom and that the evening card games were therefore part of a cosmic plan to mock him eternally for his folly and vanity.

What he seemed never to remember was that my mother usually won these games. His own part in the ritual was at some point in the evening to "shoot the moon," which meant to capture every single heart and Dirty Dora, the queen of spades, too, instead of avoiding hearts and the queen, as the three women in his life inevitably did. His contrarian strategy was supposed to surprise, defeat and even humiliate us, notwithstanding the fact that the three of us never cared very much who won anyway.

On this particular night, after my father had explained in his tone of strained patience the rules and objects of the game to my mother for perhaps the 300th time, and after we had negotiated our way through several rounds of unremarkable and defensive play, my father took a heart.

My father took this heart with his well-practiced poker face, an expressionless surface beneath which my sister and I could discern self-satisfaction and even an unnerving excitement. My sister shot me the look that meant, "He's going to shoot the moon. Again."

My father's mentality was the kind for which winning was never quite enough. In croquet he must drive your ball into the bushes. In Monopoly he would urge you to mortgage your properties rather than fold immediately. As I looked at his face that night a strange feeling came over me. An alien determination. A sense of luck, pluck and recklessness. I could feel power in my mind and in my fingers. I was going to stop him. Stop him dead. He was going to get Dirty Dora and every heart but one. I would see to it. This was as good as flying.

The ace of hearts was in my hand. I held on, resisting the impulse to discard it onto one of his tricks. I masked my child face. I waited. Power suffused me. Finally he was forced to lead hearts. He played his king. I looked at him, holding his gaze. An understanding passed between us, a recognition. He laughed.

Life changed after I dropped my ace of hearts on his king that night. In defeating him, I moved into his camp. At the age of nine, I had been initiated into the world of power. Gradually my mother and sister stopped going to the boat on weekends and stayed home; my father and I went alone, companions. Together he and I built a sailing dinghy. After that I would sail my eight-foot craft alone all day in the shipping lanes, while he would sit in the cockpit of the boat, drinking beer with old Cap and his other sailing cronies, taking the boat out less and less.

We were equals, partners in an apparently genderless world. But I was sailing my dinghy unwittingly into the choppy waters of adolescence. I began to notice other dinghies and they were without exception skippered by males. One youth with particularly long legs and dark unruly hair had lied about his age one summer to crew on a tuna boat in the Galapagos Islands. He took me to parties where the lights were low, taught me to dance close in slow, sea rhythms. With another boy I swam at night in flickering pools, learned to hold my breath in lingering underwater kisses.

My father withdrew in an ancient embarrassment, saying "no" each morning to lipstick kisses on his bristly cheeks (I was nearly grown, after all). I became more my mother's child, learning from her the secrets of heterosexual courtship, the ancient art of losing games of skill and chance by a single point. My father sold the boat, took long naps and told my mother to wake him just before I returned from school so I wouldn't worry about his growing lethargy.

On that last day, I broke the pattern of a year by kissing him after breakfast, before the school bus arrived. On the last morning of his life, I kissed him, and he let me. That's all. But it seems large.

Did we somehow both anticipate the course of that day? Did we acknowledge finally the toiling of his heart, fluid transported through steadily narrowing passageways? Did we foresee that, at six o'clock in that declining afternoon, my mother would come out of the bedroom where my father had been napping to say in bewilderment, "Girls, I can't wake up your father"?

In my mad dash down the hall from the maid's room to my parents' bedroom, I transformed myself back into my powerful child self. I might have been running across the patio with a baby blanket pinned around my neck, hurtling toward the edge and perfect flight. I knew I had the power to wake him. I alone had it.

I who had once stopped him dead with the ace of hearts could as surely raise him up.

But when I put my hands on him he was already cool, emptied out. He felt to me like some fragile, cunningly wrought and now abandoned dwelling place. In the days and weeks that followed, I kept expecting him to appear at the foot of my bed at night, holding a bag of crab claws as he had so many times before. He might telephone. Having departed his chrysalis, he must have transformed himself into something else. But what was it, this something else he had become?

In the last semester of my senior year of high school, I began to suspect he had become the student teacher in my French I class. Not literally, of course. But with the arrival, in Madame Kashishian's French class, of the young, bespectacled, scholarly man, with slightly balding head and touchingly slim wrists, my search began for the loved one who might somehow stand in for the missing one. We married the following year. I was eighteen.

At the foundation of this curious relationship was the acceptance of the principle of male privilege, by both of us. I quit school and worked while my husband attended graduate school. This was 1958, after all. If I was going to abandon my female deities, then mainstream, white, heterosexual culture would certainly support me. In due time, I was awarded a house in the suburbs, two children, and an anguished, restless heart. Not for a dozen years did I fully realize it had been a mistake to hang up my Superman cape, that the patriarchal culture which seemed to promise each woman a capable male to negotiate all the family's transactions with the world was lying through its teeth.

Somehow my own metamorphosis from heterosexual and mostly white to homosexual and mostly of color was bound up in my own growing awareness of social inequality. My heart longed for equality, for passion, for flight. The love of one woman for another became for me the very emblem of that equality.

Unfortunately in the succession of love relationships over the next twenty-five years, I was looking for the queen of hearts. Not the king of hearts, mind you; I had learned that much. But these were women who gave the certain appearance of being in charge, capable, self-sufficient, professional, determined. They might be dreamers or intellectuals or merely opinionated. But in every case I recognized the life of this person as being somehow more significant than my own. Like my mother and my grandmother before me, the only power I could lay claim to in relationship derived from the deep and unutterable conviction that the beloved depended on me in some elemental way, that her primacy–the very primacy I had recognized and validated–was therefore only apparent, not real.

Equality eluded me as an adult in the same way flight had eluded me as a child. Metaphorically my knees and elbows bore the scars. With each relationship, I dreamed of new ways to make it work, until one night, finally, I dreamed a new dream, one lighter than air itself, the dream that said solitude might be sweeter than inequality, that I was–in the final analysis–perfectly capable of taking care of myself, that in fact we all are. We are women. Glimpsing this, for the first time in my life I left a relationship without having another waiting to receive me. I bought myself a small house, a small refrigerator. I danced the dance of the happy crone. I danced myself at last into the very relationship I had so long sought.

Solitude, independence and equality were things my mother never had in her lifetime, so she could hardly teach them. Like me, she had no real models, though I do recall a snapshot of her taken in her late sixties, dancing alone at a May Day celebration, radiant, unself-conscious. We are all making this up as we go along.

We examine our legacies. From my father I claim a certain half-terrified love of travel and adventure; a dreamy creativity; a satiric sense of humor subject to excess; a curious blend of extravagance and economy; a fear of sloth; a respect for the gears of domesticity and a commitment to their maintenance; random curiosity; a sense of method; a delight in jazz; a passion for books, libraries and learning, whether formal or casual; love of hardware; a gift for Spanish irregular verbs; a fascination with vehicles and their unceasing movement. From my mother I claim a love of story; fierce compassion and empathy; commitment to family, to bravery, kindness and determination; a proclivity to soak in bathtubs; a trustful, suspicious nature; delight in color; love of quiet and solitude; a sense of the body; a belief in the Great Mother; contempt for the Pope; fatalism; touchy pride; an encyclopedic knowledge of popular music; dead reckoning in a mall; affection for plant life; a reverence for clean houses and folded laundry; the ability to hit a low and inside pitch clear out of sight.

The self I am is fashioned out of this idiosyncratic rag bag of inherited qualities, values and preoccupations. We are all familial bundles of desire and compulsion. In *Faultline*, Arden Benbow says, "I believe we choose our own metaphors, not the other way around." I choose the flying girl, the dancing crone, a few hearts.

Monkey Boy

Linda Smukler

I lift my hand to my face   my hand's the biggest thing around
and filled with rivers   it has stems I can see through to the dark
fuzzy air   I hold my hand to my face and down below I feel my
legs curl up to my chest   I look out at the door of my room   it's
open a crack and there's light   it's pink and dim   nightlight they
say   light for Daddy to see when he comes in the crack   light for
me not to be afraid   monkey's here too   I can feel his hard face
and his big ears and the straps that hold up his checkered pants
his name is Jim and he sleeps with me every night   he's here
when I'm naked   he's here when I open my eyes and my stomach
hurts and the bed is wet   he's here when I'm high on a pole stuck
right up through me and people are laughing and I can't get down
he's here and he runs on his hard curly toes and takes me away
like he'll go and get somewhere like Wyoming where I can jump
into his body and be there too   in Wyoming my name is Ace   Jim
Ace the monkey boy who can run forever and climb the tallest
trees   whose hair is dark and whose eyes can see rattlesnakes a
mile away   who has no mother or father and lives fine by himself
Jim Ace the monkey boy sleeps under the stars where the light is
blue and green and there are sometimes wolves but the wolves are
his friends   they sing to him Hello Jim Ace across the plains Hello
Jim Ace   my ears have grown larger than monkeys' ears   Hello I
shout back across the plains   then the night floats down and the
wolves come close and lie in a circle around me   where I am the
center and I sleep

Tales of a Lost Boyhood: Dolls

Linda Smukler

I sit on Sandra's bed with my horse and Sandra's dolls. The blonde Tyrolean boy rides his Pinto. I watch as they explore a cave. The Tyrolean boy picks the Norwegian girl up off the ground with a sweep of his arm. They ride off together. The boy's pet wolf follows behind the horse. The wolf protects them everywhere, through rocks and cliffs and the desert. She carries their water around her neck. The boy looks at the girl. They ride far away. Then the girl falls off the horse. "Girls!" I say disdainfully for the Tyrolean boy. I look at the other dolls. There's a Russian girl and an Italian girl, both wearing long skirts and frilly blouses. They can't go out into the desert in those things, I think. I get up and walk into my parents' bedroom to look for a comb.

Reaching high on top of the dresser, I take down Dad's jewelry box. The box is brown and flat. I press the gold button. The box opens and inside I touch the green velvet. All of Dad's treasures are here. Four sets of cuff links and a coin on a chain. Three silver dollars and a tie clip. I put the tie clip on my shirt. There's no comb. I place the box back up on the dresser and look in Dad's closet. I like the suits. Dad has lots of shoes and shirts too. The closet smells like dust. I also like the ties. I pull down a flowered one and place it around my neck. I walk over to Mom's closet where the mirror is. The door is open. Inside, it's filled with dresses. I close the door. In the mirror, the flowered tie hangs down to my knees. It makes me look like a clown. I take it off. Back in the closet there's a black-and-red tie that's as wide as my stomach. There's also a narrower one that's blue and yellow. I put that one on and take off my glasses. I get as close as I can to the mirror and if I don't turn my head, I can't see my ponytail. It looks like I have a crewcut. I almost look like Dad, but I don't know how to knot the tie. I see the comb on the nightstand. I pick up the comb and draw it through the top of my head. It gets stuck in the rubber band that holds my hair. I pull the comb out and put the tie back in Dad's closet.

The Tyrolean boy jumps off a cliff. I catch him and look into his face. He plays a trumpet. I lift my right fist to my mouth. My left hand plays the valves. I comb the boy's hair to the side. There needs to be more of him, I think. Sandra has a scissors in her desk. "OK, girls," I say, "take off your dresses." I undress the Russian, the Italian, and the Norwegian girl, and hide their dresses behind a pillow on the couch. Their panties look like bathing suits. "Get in line now," I tell them. I make the first cut on the Italian girl. Her hair falls on the bedspread. "There, that's better," I say. I cut bangs, then cut all the way around her head. Her hair sticks up all over. There's a hole where the scalp shows. I stand her up. What will Sandra say? My stomach jumps, then I tell myself she won't see. I'll make the Russian girl's hair a little longer. I cut. It doesn't look as good as I thought it would. The dolls' chests look too skinny. I wish I had shirts for them. I put the Russian girl on the black horse. There. Now the Russian girl has a new name. Her name is Jerry.

I look into one of my drawers. I've been hiding a baby doll there under my sweaters. I cut its hair a long time ago. I bring it to the bed. The other dolls look tiny next to it. The baby doll is the giant's baby and lives in a house with a big cradle. The giant has captured Jerry and his friends, Mike and Peter. The boys have to rock the cradle and feed the baby's large mouth. They pour milk down the baby's throat and it chokes. The boys have no clothes. They are cold. They will escape now on their horses. They crawl out through the cracks underneath the doors.

I hear Mom's car drive up the driveway. There's no place to hide the dolls. Sandra will know they're gone. I throw the scissors into the desk and slam the drawer. I brush the strands of cut hair off the bed and into my hand, and run to the bathroom where I flush the hair down the toilet. I hear the door open downstairs and run back into the room to try to put the dresses on the dolls. I accidentally put the Italian dress on the Russian girl. There's no time to change them. I set the dolls back up on the shelf and race into the bathroom again. I sit on the toilet. I hear the refrigerator open and close. "Practice first, then do your homework," Mom says. Sandra asks if she can have a snack and Mom tells her to take an apple. The refrigerator opens again. Sandra walks up the stairs. "Hello," Mom calls up to me. I don't answer and Mom calls again. "What?" I shout down to her. I don't move from the toilet. "We're home," she says. "What are you doing?" I tell her that I'm going to the bathroom. I take down my pants to make it seem more real. "Did you practice your piano?" she asks. "Yes," I answer. I hear Sandra walk into the room. She takes her violin out of its case. I hear the notes–A, A, D, E, G–as she pulls her bow across the strings to tune them. It's quiet now. In my mind I see her eyes scan the walls of the room. She starts to play a scale. I hold my breath. I don't know whether to get up off the toilet or not. The scale goes up and down. It stops, and the quiet lasts a long time. Then I hear a scream and running feet. The bedroom door slams open into the hall. I stand and pull up my pants. I place my hand on the doorknob. When I open the door I am the Tyrolean boy. There's a Pinto horse waiting to take me into the desert.

from *Clit Notes*

Holly Hughes

When the lights come up, the performer is sitting in a kitchen chair on the upstage right corner of the square. I recommend one of those vinyl and chrome kitchen chairs. The chair should remind the audience of egg-salad sandwiches and pickle spears.

Soon as they opened my father up, they knew. Probably knew before.

Malignant.

At first I thought: "Big deal. You have two kidneys. You lose one, it won't kill you. Plenty of people do fine on just one. Just because you lose a kidney, that's no reason to think you can't have a normal life."

If you go for that sort of thing.

Funny but this was exactly the same thought my father had when he first found out that I was a lesbian. He didn't say anything. Silence had always been his first language. But by then I was fairly fluent. I knew what he was thinking. I knew he figured he had two daughters. So he lost one. Big deal. It wouldn't kill him. Plenty of people do fine on just one. One was more than enough for his purposes. Just because he had one daughter who was a dyke, no reason to think he couldn't have a normal life.

That's all he *ever* really wanted. *A normal life.* He got pretty close. He almost had a normal life.

Do you have any idea how many different kinds of cancer there are?

Jesus! It's like all the breeds of dogs. Each with their own habits. Temperament. Preferred hiding places. Each with their own special name. The name, that's important. Because the name is the key to the future. As in, whether there's going to be a future or not.

Of course, all of them will bite. But there's a difference in how hard. There's a difference in whether they'll let you go once they've got a hold of you.

It took two weeks for the doctors to give my father's cancer a name. To tell us what disease we were dealing with. I say "we" because, when sickness enters one person's body, it doesn't just stay there. It comes to live with everyone who loves that body, its appearance determined by the kind of love you have for the body where the sickness makes its home . . .

Fuck! I didn't just say I loved my father, did I?

I meant to imply I loved his *body*.

Which is not *him*. My *father*, his *body* . . . two completely separate entities. Barely on speaking terms.

Every night we waited for my father's diagnosis, his disease would rise out of his bed and come to mine. Every night of those two weeks his disease would lie on top of me, sucking my dreams dry till I just had one dream left.

I saw a vision of the last decade in this country.

I saw a landscape of death.

A country ruled by doctors, lawyers.

This was a vision that appeared to me in white, on white.

And when I say "white," let's be clear what white I'm talking about. I'm talking about the white of the police-chalk line and especially the white of the sheet pulled over the face when all you see of the eyes are the whites.

I don't know about you but there's too many of my friends back there. Too many people who belong to me only in the past tense. So many that I start to think: "That's where I belong." At least that part of me that could say, without any hesitation:

"I want to live. In my body. In the present tense.

In front of all these people

I'm going to tell the truth."

*   *   *

Not the whole truth. Not nothing but the truth. Not that one. Just my little chunk of it. Without apology. I used to say: "I don't care who hates me."

Who did I think I was?

It's like I thought I was playing some sort of game of tag, and I was so sure that I was faster, smaller than that sweaty, balding guy we've all decided was "it." Now that part of me is somebody else I lost. Another face who appears nightly, asking to be remembered or at least counted. Promising me, if I count all the dead, I'll sleep as deep as I dare.

But there's too many of the dead to count.

So I won't sleep. What do I need with sleep anyway. Who can sleep at a time like this, huh? Besides. Getting to sleep has never been my biggest problem. My big problem is waking up.

I spent my entire childhood in a coma.

Then I turn twenty, and I kissed a woman. Sort of by accident. But she kissed me back. With a purpose. An intention I couldn't guess. Something started happening to me. Something that the expression "coming out" doesn't quite cover. In my case, it was more a question of . . . coming to.

But the world is round.

And I resent that fact!

Soon as my father said he was sick, after my father said the word "cancer," I knew I had to go home. Going home does not come naturally to me. If my father's medium was silence, mine has tended to be escape. But there's no future in escape because the world is round. So the faster you run away, the faster you end up, right back where you started, face-to-face with whatever you were running away from in the first place.

Your worst fears, they're always the most patient.

Part of my reluctance in going home, no doubt, has to do with what my parents' home is. From the outside it looks oppressively

normal. Your average, Middle-American, middle-class, middle-every-
thing split-level.

But that's just the outside!

In reality, this is the entrance to a cave . . . cave . . . cave . . .
cave . . . I know if I don't make myself as small as possible, if I'm
not willing to pretend I don't even have a body, they'll never let
me in the front door.

And as soon as I'm inside, I'll lose my footing. The floors are
always slick with a mixture of prehistoric tears, come, light ranch
dressing.

An outside light means nothing in this kind of darkness. Before I
go home, I tie a rope around my waist and give the end to my
friends:

"Don't let go of me. Don't let me fall. If I'm not back in two
weeks, come after me, OK?"

I tell everybody I'm going back because of my father. But the
truth is I'm going back because there's parts of my body I can't
feel. Parts of me still dreaming, back in my father's bed. Waiting
for some kind of wake-up call. A sign. A word . . .

OK. I'll say it.

A kiss.

Something I'm never going to get from my father. Now that he's
living with one foot in the grave and the other on a banana peel, as
he would say, isn't it time for me to wake all the way up? Once and
for all. Isn't it about time to get completely out of my parents' bed?

For two weeks I practice going home. Trying to get it right. I
get up. In the middle of the night. Crawl to the mirror. And I can
already see the toll my father's illness is taking.

I look just like the place I was born.
I'm a dead ringer for Michigan!
Can you see it?
I'm almost an island.
There's water on three sides of me.
A place carved up by ice.

The birthplace of all storms.
A short growing season.
All the cities shut down, the people moved to Texas.

I don't mean to brag. These could be my best qualities.

Step two. I try to get the woman in the mirror, the one who looks like Michigan, to repeat after me: "I want to live." A pep talk, but something goes wrong. The words swerve out of control and turn into questions. So it comes out like this:

"I want to live?
In my body?
In the present tense?
I want to tell the truth?
Which one? Mine? My father's?
Is that what I want to do with my life?"

Two weeks go by in this way. In the daylight, I conduct a futile search for the doctor who said he could get me discount Prozac if I got him season tickets to WOW. Finally my father calls:

"I just want you to know. I have the good kind of cancer."

His voice is so thin. Already. It's like the skin on the underside of arms where you can look and see–what do you know–the blood is still moving. Here's evidence that the heart's red oom-pah-pah band plays on. But it's still my father's voice. And he's talking to me in a tone I recognize, I remember. It's the one he used when I got to that age where everywhere I looked I saw snakes.

It got so bad I wouldn't go out of the house. But my father wanted me out in the world. He had done everything he could to make the world safe for me.

So he told me that there were two kinds of snakes. The good and the bad. What made the good ones good is that they ate things that were worse than any snake.

Gee, thanks, Dad. Now I had something new to worry about!

But my father assured me the snakes had everything under control. A very hardworking species, apparently. So when I saw the grass move, when I saw the darkness under the trees roll itself into the letter S, what I was seeing was a friend. Just doing his job. Keeping me safe.

"And the bad snakes, Dad? What about them?"

I had to know! He said there weren't any. Not anymore. Not in the woods we called ours. My father insisted I was safe. Nothing with teeth big enough to bite us, not in our woods. If I heard something howling at night, it was the wind. It couldn't possibly be a wolf. A coyote. Or a wolverine, ha! And the few neighbors looked just like us.

Still my father ran a thin wire around our eighty acres. Our woods. I remember him hanging up the big signs saying No Trespassing. I remember because I walked behind him. In his footsteps. Never asking what was the purpose of this fence. Who was supposed to be kept out. Who was being kept in. I couldn't imagine there was anything for the good snakes to eat. Who was lower than a snake? Just as I couldn't imagine that there was ever a time when these woods weren't ours.

I wanted to live.
In my body.
In our world.
All I wanted to be was my father's daughter.

I loved him because of his tools. His shotguns. His poison. The big sign he made, black letters on white wood: Private Property. Keep Out. Out of the corner of my eyes, I studied his hands. Massive. Like paws. The big hands of a hard worker. He was always working, so I could walk barefoot under the pines. Through our woods.

That my father has the good cancer doesn't mean he's going to live. It means there is a drug. A treatment that might, as the doctors like to say, buy him time. They like to say that, don't they, the doctors. Because they're doing the selling and not the buying of this time.

Sure, you can live without a kidney. But how long do you last without your bones, liver, lungs. Your brain. I mention these places because these are the most likely places where, even as I speak, my father's cancer is waiting, coiled out of the doctors' sight, waiting to strike again.

And so I imagine it gliding through my father's body. Starting down deep. Near the place where I used to live inside him. Moving up and swallowing what's worse than cancer. What's already hurt him more than dying ever could. Like being born in Appalachia. February 3, 1916. A family of coal miners. If they were lucky. My father and his brother Wolf grew up in the orphanage. Not because there's no family. Because there's no money. When he's twenty-five, he's the last of his kind. But now there's a little money. So he goes to a dentist for the first time. And on that first visit, they pull all his teeth.

I'm probably being dramatic. They must have left one or two. But I'm sure the cancer will get those, too.

And if this is what the doctors have promised, if this is really the *good* cancer at last, then it's bound to eat most of my father's marriage to my mother. Their terrible fights. The silences which were worse.

Until the cancer gets to the worst thing of all.

Until it gets to that thing that my father says is what's really killing him. Anybody want to take a guess what is the worst thing that ever happened to my father?

You're looking at her.

(The performer takes a little bow or curtsies.)

Fall of 1990.
We haven't spoken in several months. I'm the one to pick up the phone. At the sound of my voice, he starts to cry. Weeping. Like there's been another death in the family.

"Why are you doing this to us?"

I try to tell him I'm not doing anything. I try to tell him something's been done to me.

"Don't give me that. I watch TV. I read the paper!
You're all over the place!
This is what you wanted! You always wanted to hurt us.
You're doing a good job.
My own daughter. Act like you had no shame. No family."

I wish I had no shame. Sometimes I think that shame is all I've got. It was a synonym in our house for "family." It was the crazy glue that kept us together, and I emphasize the word *crazy*.

I try to tell my father that the person he's seeing everywhere isn't me. It's somebody's idea of me. I've become a symbol. I've been buried alive under meanings other people have attached to me. I tell him that some of what he's heard are lies.

"So you're not a lesbian?
Is that a lie?
You don't stand in front of a lot of people and talk about having sex–with women–and you call that 'art,' and then you expect the federal government to pay for it.
You never did that?
That's a lie?
That's good news."

It's my turn to be silent, but my father isn't finished.

"Could you at least stay away from that goddamn Karen Finley?
Is that too much to ask?
Homosexuality, well, that's one thing.
But people who play with their food!
What did we *ever* do to you?
Just look at yourself.

You're never going to have a normal life, I hope you know that. What was it? What happened to you? What went wrong?"

I take my father's questions seriously. I promise I will tell him what made me abandon any hope of ever having A Normal Life. I'll tell him. At least, as much as I remember.

My Father's Eyes

Tristan Taormino

I have my father's eyes. Or so people tell me. The truth is, I have a lot of him–the sensitive Irish skin; dark hair that gets peppered early with salt; sharp teeth and an even sharper tongue. When I look in the mirror now, I always see him. Not the way he looked in the end, but the way I want him to look in my mind forever. I have this black-and-white picture of him, an old headshot from his acting days, and he was definitely matinee-idol material. Even when he started going bald, way too young, he was attractive. And it was always his eyes people were drawn to first; they told everything about him. They never lied to me, never pretended, never disguised the truth. They were eyes full of love, desire, curiosity, confusion, mischief, sorrow, anger and hope.

But I don't actually have his eyes. I think people tell me that to fixate on one thing–to say they see the family resemblance. No, I don't have my father's eyes. He has bright blue eyes, blue that sparkles at you. Blue reflective glass that goes deep inside you and shows you who you are. I can see how my mother fell in love with him.

She has blue eyes, too, but they're calmer, more subtle, different than his. As the child of two blue-eyed people, I, strangely, don't have blue eyes. Something about chromosomes and recessive traits. They probably expected me to have blue eyes, but when I pushed my way out of my mom, I was already defiant. My eyes are no particular color, never the same color each time you see them. Sometimes they are pale, mossy green that turns brighter when I cry. Mostly they seem to be gray. Gray like steel beams or a smoke-colored cat. Gray like those days when you just want to stay inside under the covers.

I inherited not so much my father's eyes as his way of seeing. He's seen the projects in Red Hook, the stern Catholic School nuns in black and white, Army barracks in olive drab and mud brown. The red lips of Judy Garland in the restored version of *A Star is Born*. The pink sequins of a drag queen's dress. The creamy color of cum on a stranger's stomach. Which is like the color of his skin. And mine.

His eyes shine images of Brooklyn summers, classroom punishments, basic training, and Hollywood movies like an old film projector on a bright white wall. It's like looking through a child's Fisher Price View Finder, each image slightly blurry no matter how much light there is, each one framed with an old-fashioned white border. Sometimes the stories he tells are like looking through a kaleidoscope, repeated shapes and colors, but mixing together differently each time I look. Making new patterns out of old ones, with memories of Coney Island beaches, Irish-Catholic Brooklyn weddings, dinners with plenty of pasta and dysfunction.

His stories are also my queer history. Like so many gay men of his generation, he grew up in an openly homophobic family and was acutely aware of the homophobia of the culture at large.

The stories my father told about his mother were unbelievable- her fits of uncontrollable rage, her evil, sadistic methods of "discipline," recurring scenes of craziness and crying. In retrospect, I think she was probably manic-depressive—all the signs were there—but of course there was no awareness of mental health in that family. She was seen as domineering, as moody and often ill, but never diagnosed with any psychological disorder. They disowned each other when he came out, and they never spoke again. I never met her. She died a year after he did.

"Fags are sinners, fags are perverts, fags are bad" was drummed into his head like an unyielding techno song. He took pleasure in his sexual adventures with other boys in his Brooklyn neighborhood, but felt forced to hide his pleasure, deny it, hate it. He met other men like him in the Army, a perfect homoerotic environment, but still felt forced to remain closeted. He took comfort in the arms of sexy strangers found in restrooms, movie theaters, found in secret. He struggled for years with family violence and internalized self-hatred. I believe he married my mother in a complex web of emotion: They truly were in love, and in 1960s suburbia, when you were in love, you got married. But I also think that marrying her was a way for him to attempt to escape his desire for men.

Movies were his other great escape, from pain to a world of love and drama. He had a fantastic crush on Montgomery Clift and identified with him in his closeted torment, his tragic star quality. And he thought he was a hunk, of course. I have a photograph of Montgomery Clift and Elizabeth Taylor on the set of *A Place in the Sun* hanging above my living room couch (which was his living room couch). The photograph reminds me of his obsession with Montgomery. It reminds me of the two of us, the way Liz Taylor looks, young and happy, the way Montgomery holds her arm, so gently, but deliberately; the old Hollywood of glamour and love.

My father's past is my legacy. I am a post-Stonewall baby, Generation Q, who grew up in a time of more queer visibility, acceptance and pride than my father could ever imagine when he was my age. And I had direct access to a gay and lesbian community through my father. His was a queer world. So much of what we enjoyed together–listening to old Judy Garland albums, watching videos of The Divine Miss M in concert, showtunes and musical theater–was, to me, stuff my dad loved and I grew to love. It was only later, when I came out, that I realized his pleasures were also the tropes of gayness, but to me they were never clichés because they meant so much to him and they were such a big part of who he was. Today, my own music collection is very queer, and very influenced by my father. Madonna, The Pet Shop Boys, and The Smiths sit alongside Stephen Sondheim, Betty Buckley, Barbra Streisand.

I also had the opportunity as a teenager to live in one of the country's gay meccas. A typical child of divorced parents, I lived with my mom and saw my dad for holidays and school vacations. When I was fifteen, I spent the whole summer at my dad's, and my dad happened to live in Provincetown. I got my first job that summer, working at a leather shop, and spent my free time hanging out with drag queens and being crushed out on a dyke bike messenger named Nina. I remember grinning a lot whenever she made deliveries to our store. She had muscles and jet black hair and looked like a tough tomboy all grown up. It never occurred to me that my friends back home on Long Island weren't having a summer like mine. The summer when I wore perfume for the first time, and a transvestite named Lola helped me choose it–it was her scent and I loved the way she smelled, like spiced apples and vanilla. It was a summer of lesbian potluck dinners and five o' clock tea dances at the Boatslip.

It was a summer of walking down Commercial Street hand in hand with my father. In my memories, we are dressed in some hip outfits on our way to see Jimmy James at the Pilgrim House. Jimmy James was a performer my dad was close friends with who impersonated Marilyn Monroe. They called it "female imperson-ation," but it was really more than that. Jimmy was the most exciting, most glamorous person I knew. Unlike the tired queens with cheap shiny dresses who couldn't even lip sync very well, Jimmy sang Marilyn's songs and talked to the audience in Marilyn's voice. And his nightly transformation was magical. When I saw him during the day, he was always cute and perky and witty. When he got himself in that peach-pink sequined dress and blond wig and diamond bracelets, he *embodied* her. She was gorgeous and sexy and naughty and brash, and I wanted to be her. Not the Marilyn I'd seen in *All About Eve* with my dad, not the Marilyn on posters and t-shirts everywhere. I wanted to be the Marilyn that Jimmy was.

I also spent the summer watching my dad cruise other men on Commercial Street. He'd stop to flirt with some guy or another on the way. I can see him moving his hands a lot when he talked, fingering a guy across the ribcage, looking him right in the eye. I can see why men fell in love with him. It never felt that strange to see him with men, and even that first summer in P-Town, no one told me my dad was gay. They just assumed I knew.

I remember sitting at his kitchen table one afternoon with the younger brother of one of my father's friends. His name was John, but everyone called him Boomer, and his brother was a gay priest. "So, what do you think about your father being gay?" Boomer asked matter-of-factly.

It all came together at that moment in my head. *Right, my dad is gay. Of course, everything makes sense now. My dad is gay.* Because even through all the male roommates, the absence of any women lovers, his impeccable taste in clothes and decorating, it just didn't occur to me that my father was gay. And I was a pretty savvy fifteen year old. There was never any moment with either of my parents which began, "Honey, I need to tell you something. . . ." But my mother had gay friends whom I adored and it seemed perfectly fine that my dad was gay. Besides, he was not a typical father to begin with, regardless of his sexual identity.

My father was an overwhelming source of love, support, and encouragement throughout my life. He had the advantage, of course, of being a part-time-weekends-and-vacations dad; when I visited him, I was usually on break from school, or it was a holiday. He lived in many different cities–Boston, P-Town, Seattle, Portland, Oregon and Portland, Maine–which meant lots of exploring new cities for me. There was always plenty of shopping and good food, going to the theater, watching movies, and seeing friends. Unlike with my mother, there was little or no arguing about money, curfew, friends, rules, or setting limits because that wasn't really his job. His job was simply to love and entertain me, and he did both splendidly.

There was a recurring, unspoken ritual my father and I had which is one of my most treasured memories. When I packed for a visit with him, I always brought my best clothes, the hottest outfits, something brand new I bought just for the trip, just for him. The first morning I was there, I headed for the bathroom, showered, primped for a long time, then dressed for him. I emerged from the bathroom, strutted into the kitchen or living room, and stood there in front of him, posed for a proper look, poised for his approval.

Without missing a beat, his eyes followed my body into the center of the room, lit up with glee, and he bellowed in a loud, expressive voice: "You look fabulous!" He'd say how much he loved my dress or ask where I got the shoes, and elaborate on his appreciation. It was my moment to shine, to be the beautiful object to him. It was our moment. I relive those times now with lovers, dressing up, anticipating the moment when she will arrive at my door or I will emerge from my bedroom, and she, usually a handsome butch, will survey every inch of me, drink me in with her eyes, smile and say, "You look incredible." Sometimes, she'll even say, "You are beautiful, little girl. Come here and sit on daddy's lap."

My father loved to hold my hand in public. He loved me, wanted to show the world his affection. I used to think it was weird; I mean, no one else's father I knew held his daughter's hand so much. Then again, no one else's father dressed so well, knew all there is to know about musical theater, and owned every single Barbra Streisand album. I grew to like the hand-holding, especially as I got older. We were sometimes mistaken for a May-December romance, but, more often, people noticed that I was his spitting image. Even then, I think we still looked like we were in love. He'd take my hand in his, kiss me on the cheek, tell me a funny story, and I was completely content to walk down that road with him forever.

*   *   *

My father was my femme top role model. He was always in charge, on top, running the show. His candor and assertiveness appealed to me; I mean you always knew how he felt about something. He knew what he wanted, and went for it without a trace of ambivalence. Even when he was diagnosed, he was clear in his living will that he didn't want to suffer. "I want the morphine drip," he used to say over and over. "Give me that morphine drip." Now, my father was not low maintenance by any means, and you could say he had some, well, control issues. But he pulled off that desire for control with warmth, grace, charm, seduction and lots and lots of style. He wasn't nelly or flamboyant in the way some of my favorite fags can be, but he wasn't the butchest boy around either. He was a subtle combination of aggression and compassion, dominance and emotion, flirtation and cool distance. That's why I say femme top, and he was a fierce one.

He was also more of a feminist than any of my radical activist girlfriends and more of a nineties man than any of my sensitive-type boyfriends. He was a mouthy, opinionated political beast, and a fiery fighter for justice. Even when he got sick, he was still fighting to get the lefty, progressive United Way to offer domestic partner benefits to its employees. He had some of the best radar for bigotry, double standards and misogyny. He didn't learn about feminism in college; he figured it out in life. He saw inequality and oppression and took notice, gave it a name, tried to make sense of it. We used to have conversations that went on for hours about politics, equal rights, justice. He loved to hear about the trouble I was causing on campus, the marches I went to in Washington, the Queer Nation demos. Both my parents taught me to stand up for what I believed in and supported my activism; my father always challenged me.

My father made me the girl I am today—one who likes anonymous sex, showtunes, and well-dressed men. Not to mention butchy girlfags, Bette Midler, and leather. My mother doesn't know quite what to make of me, and neither do my lovers. My dad was no leatherdaddy, and even though he flirted with power, craved control, he never practiced S/M per se. I still think my penchant for kinky sex relates back to him. I'm definitely in it for the drama and the power play. And I do love dykes who are daddies. Fierce butch tops with slick, shiny, barbershop haircuts and shirts that button the other way. Daddies who have dicks made of flesh and silicone and latex and magic. Daddies with hands that touch me like they have been touching my body their entire lives. Daddies who have big cocks, love blow-jobs, and like to fuck girls hard.

My father passed on his wounds to me, too. I never thought there could be so much anger and sadness and rage inside one man, inside this man I worshipped, but there was. There was always lots of yelling and screaming and fighting with him. Slammed doors, dramatic fallings out. He was so dramatic, always. And he is partly responsible for the drama queen his daughter is today. Nothing was ever easy with him, and it was always intense and emotional. He was relentlessly honest about everything, and not always in a positive way. And while he was very serious about his relationships with people, they were always highly charged, overwhelmingly intense, and often came to destructive ends. I believe that my father, like his mother, was also manic-depressive or had some other mental illness, and lived for years undiagnosed. His highs were quite high, and his mania manifested as fits of rage that were some of the scariest times I spent with him. When he got sick, there was some talk about putting him on anti-depressants, but his moods were already altered by all the AIDS drugs he was on, there was really no point.

I want my father's hand holding mine again. The last time I held his hand was at his bedside. He was incoherent, barely conscious. He couldn't talk anymore, only cringe to tell me–his only daughter–that the pain was getting unbearable. I'd press the button, and when the morphine kicked in, we'd watch the tape of Barbra in Las Vegas and he'd smile. Sometimes he'd roll those blue eyes when the nurse he hated came by. Once, he squeezed my hand, and when I looked at him, he winked at me.

I want my father's eyes; I want to have those eyes now. Eyes that showed me what it was like before the big queer revolution. Eyes that sought out others like him in cities. Eyes that tried to make sense of the world before them. Eyes like mine. I want my father's eyes looking at me with love, with pride, with enchantment, the eyes of the one person who saw me the way I wanted to be seen, whose eyes showed me a beautiful, powerful woman.

I search for those eyes in crowds. On the subway, at parties, at that record store on 12th Street with the big musical soundtracks section. Sometimes I find a pair that shows me a smart ass. Or a set that sees a soul in conflict with the struggle and the smile. Sometimes the eyes spy a girl who's all mouth and legs. I'm all those things, but I want the eyes that can see *that*. Eyes that look and love and understand. My dad was such a gorgeous combination of boy and girl, and I look for that blend everywhere. My father knew and understood me in a way no one else ever has. He was my best friend, my mentor, my teacher. I was the object of his adoration and affection, and he was mine. He felt everything deeply, experiencing life by jumping right in. I am his spitting image, the charming queer girl to his boy. He instilled in me a belief that I could do anything I set my mind and heart to, the best gift of all. One that I hold close to me, one that drives me to do what I love and to succeed at it.

When they brought me in to see him after he died, his eyes were open. Looking up at the ceiling. Far away. He had this red dot on the white of his left eye, the color of Judy Garland's lipstick. I drew my fingers over his eyelids to close them, like I've seen people do on television. But it didn't work, they stayed open. Stubborn. For the first time in my life, I couldn't see into him. And he couldn't see my green eyes filled with tears. My eyes shining images of him–hyperactive, organized, controlling, radical, loud, flirtatious, queer–like an old film projector onto a bright white wall.

Blood

Bia Lowe

Fe, fi, fo, fum . . .

Start with the ocean. That primordial stew once served as the blood supply for all the world's life. Single-celled organisms wobbled through Eden absorbing the feast that bathed them, much as the cells of our tissues are served by the blood in our bodies. The soluble realm delivered the goods, then swept the wastes away.

Let's stand on some promontory, say on a cliff in California, the Pacific lifting its skirts below us, and contemplate this intimacy, how the ocean came to live inside us. The salty bouillon is still teeming with minute flora and fauna–protozoa, algae, bacteria–but more complex life has evolved here as well. Some cells have clustered together, forming larger bodies.

A kelp forest undulates in the tides. Its khaki spatulate leaves, a vast surface area, allow the maximum number of cells to access the ocean. They gobble its CO_2, its filtered sunlight, and sigh great sighs of oxygen.

Below these forests is the abalone. A community of cells has formed a pearlescent rampart around the cells of its softer interior. Marine water is pumped through holes in the shell, through tubes, and circulates around the tender mass. The abalone feeds and breathes. The ocean water, now carrying waste and respired water, is expelled through the holes in the shell.

After snatching the abalone from the bottom, the otter reclines atop the ocean's surface as though slung in a hammock, cache of abalone riding her paunch. She is a piece of work, more complex than either abalone or kelp, a megalopolis of specialized cells.

The cells of her stomach, for example, conspire in the industry of digestion, each doing its part to dissolve the gobbled abalone.

These chemists, waste management specialists, architects of elastic-
ity, are so specialized, so localized within her body, they can no
longer reach the ocean, much less feed easily from it. So the fluid
realm is housed within, blood circulates to all points of the
megalopolis, the citizens of the body are nourished within a
branching network of veins, the cells of the otter's stomach sample
the abalone, at long last. With a little sigh, the otter, bobbing on
the blue-gray water, closes her eyes and licks her lips.

Looking over the Pacific, the great kelp branches roll into curlicues,
each whorl like a Mandelbrot set. The enormous pulse of the surf
is a lullaby my satchel of blood remembers.

   I once rode in an amniotic sea. Fluid cushioned me and a great
blue vein tethered my belly to something larger than myself.
Though dimly, I can almost see my growing shape, a curled
tadpole preparing itself for a life to be lived on land. I carry the
precious fluid within now. God help me if I ever lose my five
quarts.

My father could trace some of his bloodlines across the ocean to
England, a heritage he played to the hilt, a fantasy of landed
gentry, with his brood of hunting dogs, his collection of guns, a
fondness for organ meats and hard liquor.

   In the rumpus room, where I would escape afternoons to listen
to records, a rack of antique rifles stuck out like a haunted galleon.
Crowning that rack lay his heirloom, an enormous elephant gun,
his father's before him, its gaping barrel wide enough for shooting
softballs. Those old guns were trophies, not tools, but in the living
room, where I watched *Gunsmoke*, *Combat* and *Father Knows
Best* on weekends, my father displayed his hunting guns. Inside the
glass case each shotgun stood oiled and upright, snug in a recess
of felt. A few boxes of shells were stacked in readiness on the
bottom. But more commanding than these guns was the secret

one, one that was neither for hunting nor for show, the pistol he kept upstairs in a drawer with his handkerchiefs and boxer shorts, its metal rod clean and cold against cotton.

The phallic implications of his arsenal were not lost on me, a young teenager. He was trying to erect, with the props at his disposal, a façade of potency. Inheritance had allowed him to retire young. With no job, no direction, no self-esteem, he withdrew into himself. On weekdays he wore down the threads of his armchair. The books he read seemed to absorb him, though he spoke of them to no one, not even my mother. On weekends he walked in the country, hunted, or gardened. He had painfully few words for us, though when he watched football on TV he swore at the set like a coach on the sidelines. As he got older his breathing got louder, each exhalation grunting in his throat. With strangers he grinned like a frightened animal. He was, to put it mildly, ill at ease.

For this reason he drank. Had he succeeded in his vision of maleness–had he been, say, a lumberjack, a senator or a linebacker–he might have drunk anyway. Drink was in his blood. He drank like his father before him. Wine with dinner, beer with lunch, and strong coffee, brief antidote, for breakfast. But most of all it was Early Times, one quart of it, with water, on the rocks, starting at noon, all day long. Four quarts of fluid a day. Glug, glug, glug.

Even before statisticians revealed the genetic nature of alcoholism, I knew at a young age that alcohol would claim a chunk of my legacy. How could a child of a drunk not know this? My ears were as keen as a superhero's to the tinkle of ice from downstairs, piqued to a slower, heavier kind of footfall, tuned to the thickening of mucus in his growling throat. My nose was like a bloodhound's for the vapors of uncorked booze, for the breath that smelled both honeyed and dangerous. My vision could penetrate walls and calibrate the downward slope of his scowl, the milliliters remaining at the bottom of his bottle. I genuflected to that bottle, a zealot awaiting her day of judgment.

How could I not? How could a child of a drunk escape the

dread when, say at Thanksgiving, a swallow of wine burned like
VapoRub inside her chest, and whet her tongue for a stuporous
world? How could she not reach for the bourbon sepulchre in
hopes of stealing the family throne?

For ten years I drank, like my father, like a lush. I was proud of
how much I could hold, of how well I could drive, of how quickly
and cleanly I could vomit in someone else's home. Now I thank my
asthma for putting on the brakes, for imposing a minimum, for
saving me from speeding into the void.

I love to drink, not only blood red wine, but great quantities of
fluids. Juices, teas, coffee, milk, waters. Washed down iced or
steamed, fizzy or flat, with lemon or without, at room temperature
or sucked from a frozen mass. I like to gulp drinks fast, I like to
swallow hard. I like carbonation to burn my throat, to gulp in
succession until I belch. I like to stick my nose deep inside the bell
of a glass, to smell the nuttiness of an espresso, the rosiness of a
Gewürztraminer, the nip of ginger ale. I drink fluids as though I
were in the grips of continual thirst. I drink like my father, like a
fish.

Don't get me wrong, every time I hold a glass of anything over
two percent, I know I'm gambling. Wicked Bacchus is at one ear.
The Bacchus I envision is Caravaggio's, coy, half-naked, offering up
the goblet of sensation. "It's your own blood, your own life. Taste.
Live!"

At the other ear is Carry A. Nation pointing to the rotted
corpse of my father. "It's his blood," she scolds, "don't fool with
genetics." I'm four times more likely to unlock that crypt and crawl
inside with my father, and so I listen as I cautiously sip, this time
with an inner ear, for the sound of growling in my veins.

Liver was once believed to be the seat of the soul. Jesus was
speared there, Prometheus gnawed there, oracles saw the future

opening in its pores. Alcoholics, protagonists in their own right, blow up there. If alcoholism is indeed a spiritual disorder, a need to consume the spirits missing inside, then the liver is its target, inflating like self-importance. Liver, filter of toxins, is the seat of the ego.

Booze is a kind of essence. A hothouse of roses condenses into droplets inside a beaker, so, too, moonshine, nose paint, mountain dew. Dionysus rises like a genie from the oak barrel, the corn still, the hop kiln. We drink spirits and are in turn possessed by them. Like children who spin themselves dizzy for the sheer joy of it, we need to be spun from this world, need our vision to be skewed.

There are some substances which, by the nature of their transformation, by the virtue of becoming a greater whole than the sum of their parts, are magical. Honey, for one. The reproductive juices of sage, distilled by the barfing of a few thousand bees, turn into honey. Silver brambles alchemize into sunlit fructose. Minute yeasts belch CO_2 into pockets of gluten, and the loaves rise. Or they fart into a mash of crushed grapes and after a decade the Brunello yields unexpected flavors, chocolate, black currants, thyme. This is alchemy of the least esoteric sort. One class of substance transforming into another, gas and all. Cud into Camembert. Tubers into seventy proof.

If only our blood could be like wine. Grapes into ruby port. Lead into gold. Flesh into god.

As I write this I am bleeding. I haven't been punctured, cut, torn or bruised. This isn't the sort of bleeding that causes panic. It's that here-we-go-again kind of bleeding, the monthly sacrifice-to-the-moon kind of bleeding, a would-be mother's innards proffering potential life. I'm on the rag, got the curse, riding the cotton pony. This blood's cycle, like the ocean's tides, swells and ebbs every twenty-eight days.

Menstruation begins timidly. Squeeze a smudge of burnt sienna from the tube, rub it on a clean cotton pad. In a few hours add a little alizarin crimson. By the next day pour in a quart of cochineal. After two days reverse the process. Then, poof, clean sheet of canvas till next time.

In general, menstrual blood has more viscosity than regular blood. Then there are the occasional claret globs, the clots that, as they squeeze through the os, wrench the gut more than coffee ever could.

Perhaps these details are unsavory, but isn't this my point? Blood is our most private terror, our most intimate fascination. Who among us is not held spellbound by its beacon? The bright bubble that rises when a scab is wrenched away?

Children are most intimate with scabs, most shameless in their love of gore. The knees and elbows of my tomboy days were patched with brown polka dots; I examined them with the fervor of a chimp grooming its kin. Up close scabs looked like jerky. Sometimes, especially on my knees, scabs looked like an aggregate of fudgy granules, a dark mosaic held together in a fabric of dry filaments.

Picking scabs was a lesson in patience. When they were ready, edges gave easily, lifted to a newer skin. But when they weren't, when the lid was pried open too soon and red boiled out, I pressed the scab back, hoping blood would paste the lid shut. Sometimes I preferred to tear it off anyway, to suck up the blood, my lips puckered around the spot like a leech. Blood tasted like butter cooked in an iron skillet.

A few years ago I had my wisdom teeth pulled. During the procedure, which seemed to last hours and involved a hammer, a chisel, and more hands than I thought I could accommodate, I started to bleed. The warm, slightly viscous drops tapped a rhythm in the back of my mouth and comforted me, welcomed me into my body. And when I spit into the porcelain basin, the taste of salt and iron was a rapture as deep as masturbation.

*   *   *

Staccato here. My memories are fast and sharp. I was sixteen, away at boarding school. I had been up since five, playing soccer in the rain. My clothes were slick with mud. The vice principal came up to me at breakfast and asked me to follow him into his office. His face was drawn and he fell silent as we walked down the hall. All I could think was that someone in the dorm had ratted on me for smoking. "Boy, it sure must be bad," I offered, smiling, hoping to defuse the reprimand sure to come.

My brothers stood up as we walked into the office. It must be real bad, I said to myself, though I already knew. Their pained expressions, the thunder of my father's rages, his empty bottles of Early Times, the Colt among his underwear.

The whole drive home I kept asking them why, as if I didn't know, as if I hadn't always known. Peter offered, "Sometimes people get themselves into the grip of a vise, and they don't know a way out." He spoke those words as though he had memorized them long before and had saved them just for that moment.

Mother said she had heard a sound like a door slamming, then thought, no, not a door, something else. When she opened the door she saw him slumped, a streak of red on the wall, a second of red, a blur of something red and she quickly closed the door. By the time I got home the blood was gone, rubbed away, only a hole that tore the fabric of wallpaper in a corner of the ceiling. Had he tasted the barrel? Did he close his eyes? Had bits of his head, like Kennedy's, been torn off? How many hours did it take to scrub away the evidence? How long had my mother paced while I was away sleeping or playing soccer in the mud?

Away at school I had been free, not the sleep-deprived sentry of my household, the watchdog chained to the liquor cabinet. Away at school I was no longer a scholar of thuds and shattering glass. Over cold scrambled eggs I said, "I was mean to Daddy, I should have been nicer." I had, in fact, steeled myself against him. Opaque as glacial ice. Richard countered, "So? He was mean to you, too." His response fit, though it, too, seemed rehearsed for this moment, a reply saved for his own moments of doubt.

Guilt continues with me, as it did when he was living, a stain I can't seem to wash away.

A garnet drop, a pomegranate seed, a pool of horror. A badge of courage, a declaration of war, a plastic bag suspended above the body.

History runs inside it. It screams for justice, challenges detergents, points the finger. Shed without mercy, it can run in the streets, seek its own vengeance. Contracts with the devil are signed in it. It's a vampire's rhapsody. A mosquito's empire. A person can develop the taste for it. It is thicker than water. It carries the virus.

A ruthless thirst. It can be found on one's hands, on the saddle, in a bank. Virile when red, upper crust when blue. An excitable ingredient, made to boil or curdle, run hot or cold.

A fellow, a black male, an L.A. gang. It is paired with thunder. It can mingle and make its own bonds. A sausage, a pudding, a sensitive hound. A curse, a bath, a legacy, an ocean.

In a drawing of a family tree in which I am the trunk, underground roots branch below me and splay into infinitesimal hairs, unknown lineage, imperceptible parts of my construction. Were there maniacs among those ancestors? Flagellants? Cannibals? Does their DNA whisper in my veins? And closer to the stem, the kin with names and well-known maladies, are their messages louder in my blood? There were, I know, diabetics, heartless insurance salesmen, a manic-depressive, a convict who died of tooth decay. Will they become me? Will a summons in my blood banish me to the same path as my father, as god-knows-who-else down there in the dark earth with him?

In middle age I still succumb to the bloody rites of fertility, though by now the chance of my having babies has ebbed. This trunk rooted in ten thousand years of genetic material will not bear fruit. Blood, each cell bearing its cargo of DNA, will not make a home for new life. That's all folks, end of the line. Above that trunk are bloodless invisible branches. This is one.

Many years ago, I stood on a cliff at Point Lobos and stared at a finger of the Pacific as it nudged the inlet below. The kelp was doing its show of psychedelia, paisleys heaved among the sequins. Sea lions barked and cool air stung my cheeks. My father's ashes had been in the ocean for a few months, his meager ounces mixed with the megatons, more carbon added to the soup. We are different people, I reminded myself. For one thing, I'm alive.

Yet still when I look at my face in the mirror I see my mouth weighed down by his scowl. A shroud of insurmountable failure, his, threatens to swallow me whole. It's a ghost story a frightened child can't shake, even in middle age.

My antidote, that crucifix I hold up to ward off such monsters, is an image of the Pacific, the cliff at Point Lobos, its surf seething below me. And to match that image, I add a little voice-over, recite a childhood rhyme, something I've saved for moments like these, "The world is so full of such wondrous things, I'm sure we should all be as happy as kings." It's too cheery a reflex, I suppose, like whistling in the dark, but it calms my pulse.

Blood drums in my ears. So like the ocean, teeming with its component creatures, red cells, white cells, leukocytes, T's. Cells that nourish, or cells that protect. Some that seal the wounds.

Distance

Karin Cook

Once I stopped doing things he could easily videotape, my father lost sight of me. Admittedly, my activities never really made for good film. I didn't play on teams or perform on stage. My path was marked by paper, rather than medals or trophies; my small accomplishments, mainly academic, were stored in files, not displayed on shelves or viewed on a screen.

I was the daughter of divorced parents; my mother and father had parted when I was two. In the early years of weekend visits, my father, a pilot by profession, recorded all arrivals and departures with his video camera. In every shot, it seemed, I was waving. As he tinkered with batteries and pressed buttons, my life passed by. I always felt that somehow in spite of his presence throughout my childhood, the real me–my developing heart and mind–remained invisible.

To my knowledge, none of that footage has ever been rewound. Instead, the videotapes, labeled and dated in his block-lettered handwriting, are neatly stacked in the cabinet under the television. They signify that yes, in fact, he was there. But unwatched, silent in their boxes, they beg the question: What did he see?

In contrast, my adolescence was spent as a spectator to his athletic travails and triumphs, as he participated in a range of endurance-testing events. He began with the occasional 5 or 10K road race and worked his way up to marathon distance. At many of these races, I was there to watch and record his accomplishments. I knew that to capture my father moving on film, I must move with him, anticipate his speed, know where he will go next, have studied his course. If I stood still, held my own ground, his motion would blur before my eyes.

After eleven marathons, my father switched gears and began biking. At 58 years of age, he completed his first Ironman Triathlon–2.4 mile swim, 112 mile bike, and 26.2 mile run–in under 14 hours. That year, I flew to Kona, Hawaii to bear witness as he tested himself against the grueling 140.6 mile course. My role was to document each phase of the competition. I had listened closely to his minute-mile analysis and approximations. I knew where to be and when.

A mile before the finish, I recognized my father in the distance. I knew his shape against the world from years of watching. His posture embodied determination, his stride signified independence. I watched through the tiny screen, hoping to see myself reflected somewhere in him. As my father raced by, I felt that initial high–a cheer rising within me–and was struck by the recognition that for an instant we were both in the same place, held together for as long as I could keep him in focus. Then he was gone like a flash.

That feeling of being passed by made me long for motion. I took off running beside him. My father later said it was the instinct of an athlete and encouraged me to "go for it." I feigned boredom, but something surged deep within me. It was the hope, perhaps, that if I donned the neon lycra and reflector panels, he would finally see me.

Not surprisingly, my decision to run the New York City Marathon had more to do with metaphor than mileage. As I set my mind on race day, I imagined a new kind of connection with my father. I hoped that by entering the world of athleticism and matching him mile for mile we might gain a common language with which to communicate. As in the Greek legend, for which the marathon is named, I longed for my journey to carry a message.

Race day was the coldest in New York Marathon history. With a November wind-chill of 17 degrees, I set out before dawn to board the bus to the Verrazano Bridge with layers of sweats and a garbage bag pulled over my body for warmth.

After a lifetime of waiting on the sidelines, suddenly I was standing at the start. Although my father came to watch me run the marathon, he anticipated a quicker pace and missed me at the designated meeting place. By his own admission, my father does not like to watch. Nor does he wait well. When finally I caught up with him, five boroughs and 25 miles later, he was standing in Central Park amidst the spectators.

"I have to go," he announced, checking his watch. "I hadn't expected you to take so long."

I couldn't speak, dizzy with exhaustion, having saved only enough energy to go that last mile. I could barely lift my arm to wave as he snapped a photograph.

"Next time you'll just have to train harder," he called out in a motivational tone and then raced off to his car.

He hadn't meant to be mean. Anticipating the next event has always been the consolation he offers as he takes flight. By the time I crossed the finish line, arms outstretched in triumph and wrapped in a silver space blanket, my father was already miles away.

Running a marathon requires a dozen acts of will. It is a 26-mile dialogue with determination. The biggest challenges are not always the most obvious. It should have been enough that my father came to support me. He waited all day in the cold, charting the distance, hoping to cheer me on. As an athlete, he believes in breaking records, is focused outward in his desire to compete and achieve. Given that orientation, his absence at the finish line felt symbolic.

Perhaps because the finish is the point at which expectation meets accomplishment and hope gives way to truth. Standing in the reunion area with a finisher's medal around my neck, I realized that mileage amassed does not necessarily bridge distance.

Now I run almost every day. I put on my lycra shorts, running shoes, and jog bra. But I never call myself an athlete. I run to rid my body of stress, to meditate. I stop and walk when a bright leaf or bird catches my eye. And while I lust after those long, sinewy muscles found on real runners, I am not interested in balancing my electrolytes or keeping track of my pace.

Ultimately, I am committed to process over product, a daily

practice which honors determination, but leaves room for detours. Amidst the pounding of my sneakers on pavement and the rhythm of my breathing, I have discovered a kind of quiet–a still, solitary place in which to reckon with distance. I have learned that sometimes it is as important to stand still as to move forward, to listen rather than watch–not for the applause of others, but for the enormous murmur of my own voice.

Mulberry Tree

Zelda Lockhart

My Uncle Leland looked like my father–the same lean, six-foot-four body, except Deddy had big, bulging muscles and was getting a beer belly, and Leland was thin and muscular like a runner.

I remember Leland with a bloody face, blood that stained and dyed brown the cement steps of our front porch, like the crushed-mulberry stains on the cement steps in the alley. Deddy had stabbed Leland–"in self-defense," Mama said over and over on the phone.

The kids didn't go to the funeral, and when the adults returned for food, I felt guilty. I couldn't believe that they came back to our house. Deddy had killed their father, uncle, brother, son. Leland was dead and his frozen blood was stepped on by funeral shoes entering the killer's house. Maybe they thought the stain was mulberry.

The stain was there months later, after the cold cement steps had thawed and dried from the heat.

That year I turned nine and the house two doors down burned up, leaving a vacant lot, a set of three cement steps that led from the alley to the missing house, and a mulberry tree that must have been growing in that back yard for years. As many times as I had gone down the alley, I had never seen that tree before.

As the summer droned on, I forgot what the lot had ever looked like with a house. On weekends the lot became our baseball field, run-across field, football field, and milkweed-fight field. The lot: a mulberry tree, a field of buried broken glass, and three cement steps that we used as a recovery box whenever someone would get the wind knocked out of 'em.

118

In July Mama and Deddy reopened Leland's tavern and his neighborhood grocery and renamed them Blackburn's Bar & Grill and Blackburn's Market. Mama ran the store on one corner of Delmar and St. Louis Avenue, and Deddy ran the tavern across the street. That summer we went from being a family of ten who traveled in an old Country Squire station wagon–with a constantly falling-off muffler and parts frequently removed by Deddy when he was drunk and not wanting Mama to escape his punches–to a family of ten who owned a new black Cadillac and a white van with a desert landscape on the side.

For the rest of the summer Mama and Deddy kinda disappeared and I had to stay home with Benson, Daryl, and Jessie while Towanda and Lamont went to marching-band camp, and LaVern and Roscoe worked in the store. Every morning I made breakfast for three, dressed them, and put them in the back yard, Daryl and Jessie in the playpen so they wouldn't fall into the basement hole. I'd go to the basement, put a load of clothes in the washing machine, bring up the load that was taken off the line the night before, and iron in Mama's room while I watched *Felix the Cat*, *Happy Days*, and *The Young & The Restless*. Then I'd make two sandwiches with two cookies on the side and a bowl of ABC soup for Jessie. I'd change Daryl's and Jessie's diapers and give them all a nap on the floor in Mama's room where the air conditioner kept it cool.

When I was sure they had fallen asleep and the one-hundred degree sun was just about to reach the clothesline, I'd go out to the pole, with its diamond-shaped web of lines and steel, and hang clothes. Then I'd go in and make my own lunch–garlic baloney with lettuce (if we had any) and mustard on bread, and two sandwich-creme cookies. I'd sit in the kitchen, checking past the door to Mama's room to see if the little bodies had sat up on their pallets.

My loneliness was like the loneliness I felt when I was four. That year all the big kids were in school, and Mama was always tired with Benson growing in her belly. She napped almost all day, leaving me waiting for the mailman's footsteps on the porch and, later, the sound of the school bell.

I knew I would feel less lonely if I took down the clothes and washed and hung another load, but instead I sat at the kitchen table, which I'd cleaned with a dishrag that smelled like Palmolive, eggs, and bacon grease. Through the back door I could hear kids playing in the shade or in the water at the fire hydrant. Two doors down I could hear Angela and Denise yelling at their little brother and sister, who were also pinned in the house till their mother got home from work. At least I could go out back to hang clothes. Their voices made me long for 5:30 when Mama closed the store and the world came back to keep me company.

Before long, Daryl, who was always cross, would start crying, or Jessie would start blowing spit bubbles, or Benson would start lifting and banging his leg, and the worst part of the day was over. I could put them out to play on the back porch, where the only shade hovered long enough for me to put up the child gate and the play pen and watch my story while Pledging and Windexing. The closing music to *The Guiding Light* made me feel empty, like air was filling my belly. I had an hour and a half to finish cleaning, take the dinner meat out of the freezer, and put the clothes away before Mama got home. I timed myself by seeing how much I could do in the time my wooden Fisher Price clock could play its tick-tock song. I'd wind it over and over as I went from room to room.

Mama only let me go to the store one day that summer–she made LaVern stay home. Mama had always said I was better off watching the boys than getting in the way. "You too young to really help by ring'n up things on the cash register. Besides, I don't want you down here eat'n up all the profit." So when I did go, I sat on a stool behind the counter and ate up all the profit.

That day I ate as much as I could in Leland's old store. Whenever Mama would go to the meat counter to slice baloney or Braunschweiger, and Roscoe was sweeping, I snatched a bag of Fritos off the clip and a Hostess cupcake off the shelf. I took a handful of corn chips and a big bite of cupcake, just getting the salt and chocolate mashed up enough to swallow. The back of my throat was getting scratched by the chips, but I hurried and filled my mouth again. I did the whole snack in three mouthfuls, and I had five snacks that morning.

At lunch time Mama had Deddy cross the street from the tavern to watch the store while she ran me home. I insisted that I was still hungry and took home a baloney sandwich. For some reason she didn't hit me or yell, just kept her eyes on the road and said, "I cain't have you eat'n all the profit."

The only time Mama hit me that summer was the Saturday I came running in from playing on the lot with a fireball jawbreaker stuck in my throat. She set the pressing comb back on the eye, punched me in the back, and kept pressing Towanda's hair. I went back to the lot and hid in the mulberry tree, waiting for Angela or Denise or somebody to come back out and play. The branches were thick and low, the trunk was thick and sturdy, and the layers of branches went high enough for me to see backyards and the tops of garages. I saw Mama come out on the back porch and yell for me, and I ignored her. I knew she couldn't see my brown face and legs mixed up in those dark green leaves, brown-gray limbs, and black-purple berries. I wasn't going to go in so she could make me feed the baby or sweep up the hair, saying, "When ya see someth'n that needs done around here–do it." And then she'd get ready to leave for Saturday night at the tavern, and I'd be stuck.

When no one came back to the lot to play, I ate mulberries, and when I felt like puking mulberries, I threw some, trying to hit the top step of the three cement steps. When I had made a stain as big as the one on our front porch, I climbed down and wiped off the seeds and put on a little dirt, then brushed it off to make the stain look dry. I tried walking up the steps without noticing the stain. I smiled and walked and talked like I was greeting someone at their front door. Every time I stepped on the stain, I heard Leland's head hitting, cracking on the top step, and felt the rubber of my Betsy Wetsy doll puncture under the pressure of my fingernails. Still no one came out to play. So I played until Leland fell through the glass of the front door, pieces of broken glass falling, muted. I played until Leland got up to run and no sounds were carried by the bottoms of his shoes, his hands and knees grinding in glass on cement. I played until Deddy's knife connected under Leland's chin, and Leland fell back. His head did not hit and make a cracking noise like Christmas nuts in Mama's palms, but hit the top step and bounced off, the knife spinning in blood.

Black, polished shoes had stepped on the stain, over and over, and come into the house to cry with Mama and Deddy, and I felt so guilty. All of the people my father called family, but who we rarely saw, were in our house. Some of them lived right here in St. Louis, some even in our neighborhood, but we never saw them either. These people were at our house after the funeral and Deddy only went to jail for one day, so he was at the house, too.

Leland's oldest daughter was bending over a kitchen drawer, asking me where the knives were. Her skirt was black lace with a hem that came only to her butt, and she was wearing black fishnet hose and no underwear.

The sound of stainless steel came back, unmuted–my cousin finding a good knife and sharpening it on Mama's stone, the knife hitting cold cement, which turned red then brown. She stared at me. My eyes were fixed on her hand and the knife, and I wondered how her velour black heels could have stepped over the brown stain.

Processions

Cheryl B.

In memory of Robert Burke

It is midnight and your father is still alive. Outside the window, a harbor glistens seamless like a sleek black dress hanging onto ethereal curves. Your eyes travel from the harbor to the bed, trying to figure why such a landscape awaits beneath this place. His mouth hangs open as if he has seen something shocking. You imagine what thoughts someone brings with them here. This is not the first time you have tried to get inside his head.

In him lies a tumor twice the size of you when you were born. The doctor says it weighs sixteen pounds and you imagine two infants entangled beneath his flesh. He has aged 25 years in the last six months, the thick black hair frosted gray and brittle. You reach out to touch it and expect him to flinch. He is past this now as his lungs pump out the last breaths. You begin to count them–1, 2, 3. You wonder how long it takes a body to go cold after this rhythm stops.

The chair you sit on is vinyl and spills over with foam stuffing. Your fingers tap the armrest. His favorite song enters your head, the one about the still of the night.

The silence between you and him is familiar. You question if such absence can be missed in the end, if this awkwardness will never leave, even when he does. The air is hot and sticky, the breeze trapped in humidity. The blinds shuffle in the window at half past twelve. You realize it is Independence Day and the fireworks explode in your head.

Somewhere, arrangements are being made. Messages are being left. Your cats are being fed. Your mail is being collected. Somewhere, your lover's knee is being fondled. His hair is being

123

ruffled by your best friend's other best friend. As you make a bed of the stuffed vinyl chair, he makes a bed with her. The next day she will call, asking if there is anything she can do to help you out. And for months to come this fucking and the fading will lap together in the bitter pool of your mind.

You can see your father over your shoulder, holding a wrench in one hand and your training wheels in another; he smiles and lets you go. When you were four, he gave you a bloody nose when he drop-kicked you up a flight of stairs, your face smashing into the top step. When he taught you how to swim, he told you never to turn your back on the ocean; that the sea was a beautiful and scary place, commanding attention and respect; that life could change with the shift of the undertow; that waves could wash over everything eventually.

Later he will call you *Fatso, Dummy, Stupid.* He will try to control you with words and you will intimidate him with vocabulary, putting together phrases he won't even try to understand or repeat at the docks to his co-workers. One day, during a TV news show focused on father/daughter rape, he breaks the silence when he says, "You know, I'd never do that to you."

"I know, Dad," you answer and go back to washing the dishes.

When you try to slit your wrists, he will beat you until you are both covered in your blood like you shared in some sort of ritual. But none of this matters here.

Three a.m. The catheter bag almost full with a liquid the color of a yellow-red sunrise he can no longer see. You think about the body, this delicate machine; the aspirations of a Florida retirement, a life spent in overtime, waiting; how he gambled his soul on a dream he was fed like corn flakes and ended up with nothing but a coffee can full of OTB winnings and a body full of cancer.

You picture him on the docks in his cap and wool shirt. He

called himself a *stevedore*, a word you've heard only from him and Walt Whitman. Once he told you he wanted to be a songwriter, but the ideas got jumbled in his head. The next day, you will be asked to write the eulogy. Stumped, your song is silent and daunting and only you can hear it.

The others will find this problematic: "He sent her to school to be a writer and she can't even write a eulogy!" You have always been the black goat. They get their farm animals confused. You, with the pasty white skin and the college degree.

Five a.m. You think you can see him move, but your eyes are playing tricks. His hands lie cold and alone, stiff to the touch. You wonder if death comes in waves, capturing one part of you at a time. They say the last thing to go is the hearing. You talk to him, tell him about the view from the window; how sailboats glided easily over the water earlier, made parting circles that resonated fiercely as if they were each saying, "I'm sorry." You talk in similes and metaphors. He can no longer complain of the fancy words.

It is now that the pacing begins. You move from window to bed, from bed to door. You sit in the chair. You get up. You arrange the bed sheets. You touch his forehead. You wipe the saliva from the corners of his mouth. You look at him and you can't say anything. You have inherited this trait from him, this silent resilience.

Seven a.m. The sun peeks through the blinds. In one hour the others will arrive. This hour will fill the space. This hour will be the telling hour. This hour is the last hour you have to understand, love and forgive this person. This hour you will remember always. This is the first time you have seen him without that look of disgust on his face, shaking his head, hearing him repeat, "I don't know, I don't know, I don't know."

You want to tell him you would rewrite his life if you could. You concentrate on the waiting, the fading. A nurse appears behind you. She puts her arm on your shoulder, gently pulling you away. It's time to change the I.V.

Conversations with My Father

Christian McEwen

> *In my drowned father's empty pocket*
> *there were nine dollars and the salty sea*
> *he said I know you my darling girl*
> *you're the one that's me*

–Grace Paley

1.

My father died on 18th May, 1980. I was living in California at the time, and that was the day Mount St. Helens blew up, hurling rock and ice and ash and poisonous gases twelve miles into the air, and clogging beautiful Spirit Lake with debris. Flying back to Scotland for the funeral (*racing* back, as if I could cheat the clock even then, and somehow make it home before he died), I carried with me the latest edition of the *San Francisco Chronicle*. Blazoned across its front was a full color picture of the erupting volcano. I was obscurely comforted by the devastation it had wrought.

My father. Papa. We never called him "Dad" or "Daddy," although at times I used to wish we had; Papa sounded odd and old-fashioned to me as a child. No one else called their father that. "Can I call you Daddy," I asked him once, "like the girls at school?" "If you like," he said. I tried, valiantly, but the name refused to stick. Still, I understood quite clearly that he *was* a daddy. *Dance for your daddy*, sang our Scottish nanny,

> *Dance for your daddy,*
> *My little lamb.*

127

You shall have a fishie
On a little dishie,
You shall have a fishie,
When the boat comes in.

The tenderness of those diminutives brings him back: the tall man in the shabby tweed jacket and the gray trousers, his chestnut-colored shoes tipped with tiny decorative holes. We lived in Wiltshire then, and he was commuting back and forth to London every week, working as a barrister in the city law courts. I remember the glamour of his arrival on a Friday night, the briefcase and the newspaper and the heavy overcoat, the rich grownup smell as we reached up to hug him and be twirled around. If we were lucky, he would have smuggled in some "magic putty"–a sticky pinkish substance which could be stretched and bounced, cracked and shattered, and yes, magically reconstituted. After my sister Kate and I got it matted in our jerseys and tangled in our long fine hair, our mother told us strictly that it was forbidden. But Papa brought it anyway, delighting in our pleasure, and unconcerned as always with minor domestic requirements.

He was our big brother, our rebel emperor, a wonderfully skillful grownup child, who made sketches for us with his strong-smelling Spanish felt pens, and allowed us to bounce up and down on the four-poster bed in his study. We played shipwrecks, I remember. The carpet seethed with sharks. I was supposed to look like him: the same dark hair and heavy eyebrows, the same greeny-gray eyes. I was proud of this resemblance. "You grow more like your mother every day," my Aunt Clare told me when I was four or five. "And more like my father every night," I answered promptly.

There is a photograph of the two of us taken in the early sixties, with a child's pram tilted in the background and a tumble of broken packaging. Papa and I are crouched together in the front of the picture, trying to mend something or put something together, it isn't clear which. He is wearing his favorite jacket, with the brown leather binding at the cuffs, and I'm in a gingham dress and a little woolen cardigan. Who took that photograph? My mother? Uncle Patrick? Neither of us even bothers to look up.

I'd been born in 1956, and there were three younger ones by then: Katie, born in 1958; James, born in 1960; and Helena, born in 1961. The nursery was crowded with the paraphernalia of babyhood: a tin bath with folding metal legs, tiny garments airing on a railing by the fire. Perhaps because of this, I spent a lot of time outside. I rode my blue bike on the crunchy yellow gravel, made secret hide-outs in the space behind the hedge. I remember wandering for hours in the woods behind the house, coming home dreamy and dirty and happy and exhausted.

Those woods were important to my father, too. He made up a story for us, about a family of children called Charlotte, Edgar and Bim. They were always having adventures, creeping off to the woods at night while the grownups were asleep, laden with delectable provisions. There'd be cold roast chicken and tins of sardines, a big hunk of bread and crumbly cheddar cheese. Eventually, they set up house in a hollow tree, where nobody could find them. I *adored* this trio. When Mama tried to teach us Scripture, and Kate did better than me, I flounced out of the room in a rage. "I don't want to be a pious church image," I said. I wanted to be Charlotte when I grew up, or maybe even Edgar, to fish for trout and grill it over an open fire, to own a pocket knife with thirteen different blades.

Some of these dreams I was able to realize. There were picnics by the river Avon, just across the road from our house, and holidays in Scotland, where I learned to fish. By dint of much swapping and saving and persuading, I did eventually accumulate a tremendous collection of knives. "Behaving like a boy" (like Edgar, like my father) was rather harder to achieve. I knew it was important not to whine or be a cry-baby. But Papa's boisterousness could be overwhelming. I still remember the day he ducked me in the Mill Pond, the times he tickled me (much too hard), and the terrible games of "Cold fish mousse" or "Treacle" he invented. "CO-OLD FISH *MOUSSE!*" he'd announce out of the blue, trapping one of us in his long arms and pretending to smear us all over. Then slowly and lugubriously, and with different, stickier gestures, "TREE-EE-CAL!!"

At night, too, he would loom over our beds in the half-dark, groaning out an ancient ballad in the most sepulchral tones:

> Oh WHO will o'er the Downs with me
> Oh WHO will with me ride?
> Oh who will o'er the Downs with me
> To WIN A BLOOMING BRIDE?

"Stop it, Papa!" we'd whimper, as his voice descended deeper and deeper into the hollow boom of "bride." "Oh Papa, please!" It was bedtime, and we were supposed to go to sleep. But Papa was inexorable:

> Her FA-ther he has LOCKED the door,
> Her MO-ther keeps the KEY,
> But NEI-ther BOLT nor BAR shall keep
> My OWN TRUE LOVE from me.

As I remember it, that verse always culminated in a terrifying lunge–the thwarted lover reaching for our throats–while we squawked and wriggled and tried to pull back under the covers.

It is easy to misinterpret such scenarios. But certainly this drama was *intended* to be pleasurable, even when it hovered on the edge of that bed-wetting torment, of being teased just past one's last endurance. In any case, I tried to bear it sturdily. I was the eldest, after all. And I was a tomboy, too, an honorary boy. I didn't want to let my father down.

2.

Papa was born on June 23rd (Midsummer Night's Eve) in 1926, the second in a family of seven children. His full name was Robert

Lindley McEwen, but he was almost always known as Robin, or, occasionally, "the Waa." There is a photograph of him at eighteen months or so, crowing loudly into the face of the camera, and flourishing a silver trumpet. He looks sturdy, forthright and utterly determined.

My grandfather was a landowner and Conservative M.P., and my father grew up between two family houses: Marchmont, on the east coast of Scotland, and Bardrochat, on the west. As a boy, he was quite outrageously naughty. He broke his glasses and flushed them down the lavatory. He cracked an egg over the cook's head. He threw all the nursery china down the lift shaft. Such outbursts seemed both dangerous and enviable. *What made him do such things?* I used to wonder. But no explanation was ever given. At seven or eight, he and the other boys were sent off to England to be educated. They attended a small prep school in Sussex, and were sent on, one by one, to Eton. At home during the holidays, they went fishing in the local rivers, learned to shoot. It was a shabby, old-fashioned, upper class country life, not vastly altered by the advent of the Second World War.

A photograph survives from the summer of 1942, with my father, his five brothers and his younger sister all lined up together on a wall. Papa has just turned sixteen. His arms are folded across his chest, and he looks out from under his dark brows with a wry, puckish expression. *I'll put up with this for now,* he seems to be saying, *but not for too much longer.* Unlike all the rest, he does not smile.

After he left Eton, my father completed two years' National Service, serving with the Grenadier Guards in Germany. He went on to Trinity College, Cambridge, where he won a starred First in classics and law. His charm and his intelligence were legendary; he was handsome, enthusiastic, full of promise.

And yet it was during those Cambridge years that the moody explosions of his boyhood began to reappear. There were frightening bouts of melancholy, too. His brother John Sebastian remembers him hunched on a sofa in the drawing room, talking aloud to himself, completely oblivious to all the other guests. No one in the family had any words for such behavior. It was another decade before the truth emerged: My father suffered from bipolar disorder, otherwise known as MDI or manic-depressive illness.

Without the benefit of this diagnosis, his gloomy spells were seen as an understandable response to overwork, while his manic episodes were praised as energetic and inspired. Few people realized how powerfully mood and character were intertwined, least of all himself, or the young woman who was about to become his wife.

By the early fifties, when he met my mother, Papa was well launched on a professional career, working as a barrister at the Inner Temple, London. In later years, he spoke with fondness of their courtship, emphasizing Mama's shyness, her astonishing beauty. He used to borrow a sports car from his friend Gavin Maxwell, and carry her off on long weekends into the country. I picture the two of them sitting under a tree, with a red chequered cloth spread out in front of them. There's a loaf of French bread and some good pâté, a bunch of grapes, a bottle of white wine. My mother has her back to me; I only see the rich gloss of her hair. But my father looks like the oil painting I remember from childhood: a dark, angular figure in an open-necked blue shirt, his chin propped idly in his hand. This is the romantic Robin whom I never knew, the one who painted the apple tree that hung, bright clots of color, over Mama's desk, the one who owned Chekhov's *Short Stories* and Rilke's *Letters to a Young Poet*, and scrawled his name inside them, spiky and illegible.

My parents were married in September 1954, when she was nineteen and he was twenty-eight. They set up house at 60 Drayton Gardens, off the Fulham Road, in London. Kate and I were both born there. In 1959, the family moved to Coneybury, a sturdy thatched house less than a mile from Stonehenge. For five years, we lived there very happily. Then, in 1964, we moved again, to Marchmont, my father's boyhood home in the Borders of Scotland.

3.

Marchmont was beautiful and spacious and dilapidated, a big pink sandstone house at the end of a long avenue of beech trees. There were several thousand acres of land, used mainly for growing wheat and barley, and as pasture for the sheep. On the surface, at least, it was an idyllic place to live. Unfortunately there was never enough cash to keep it up.

Because English law cannot be practiced north of the border, our move to Scotland had essentially cost Papa his professional identity. He might have commuted to London as he had done from Wiltshire, or taken on some teaching work in Edinburgh. Instead he decided to follow in his father's footsteps, standing as Conservative candidate for East Edinburgh in 1964, and again for Roxburgh, Selkirk and Peebles in 1965. But plagued by his first really serious bout of manic depression, he lost both seats. For the next eleven years, much of his income came from entertaining rich Americans during the shooting season. It was a sad come-down for a man as able and ambitious as he'd once been.

At eight I understood little of this, except that Papa seemed to have more time now that we lived at Marchmont. I followed him around outside, down by the river Blackadder. He bought me a rod of my own, with a good reel, and an album in which to keep track of all my catches. As a "non-birthday present" (one of his specialties) he also presented me with a book called *A Boy Goes Trouting*. I was very proud of this, though the text itself was dry and hard to follow. It was as if he had given me the keys to his private kingdom: *This is how a girl becomes a boy. And this is how a boy becomes a man.*

The summer I was nine, he rented a house from his friend Gavin Maxwell, author, by then, of the best-selling *Ring of Bright Water*. It was set on Isle Ornsay, a tidal peninsula off the coast of Skye. There was a tall whitewashed lighthouse, two converted cottages, and a tousled garden filled with meadow grass and roses. I loved this place. Kate and I spent hours hunched over the rock pools, watching hermit crabs. We set up shops on the strand, selling fragments of glass and pottery and colored shells. My mother provided all of us with holiday scrapbooks, and I crammed mine with wildflowers, carefully labeling each one in heavy pencil: *Ragged Robin, English Stonecrop, Tormentil.* Papa drew pictures for me on demand: a wonderful blue lobster, a lurid green crab with scary claws.

He was happy there, I think, visiting Gavin on his boat, the *Polar Star,* checking the lobster pots, tramping across the ribbed sand back to Skye. But the recovery was only temporary. By the time my brother John was born, in November 1965, Papa was once more in the grip of a serious depression. Years later, I learned the story of those early weeks. "I *hate* that baby," he announced to Mama as she sat breast-feeding. "I *hate* that baby!" Between 1964 and 1977, he was hospitalized some fifteen times.

What kind of help was available to him then? My mother tells me that he was subjected nine times to ECT (electroconvulsive therapy), though only once did he follow through with the prescribed medication. He had a great contempt for psychiatrists and psychoanalysts, and for the most part refused to meet with them. However, he did agree, reluctantly, to take lithium. It was only introduced in 1970, and for a number of years the therapeutic and the toxic dosages were extremely close. Was Papa told of this? Did he have any side effects? For example, was he still able to read? Did his hands shake when he wanted to draw?

I would love to know the answer to such questions. But in those days I didn't even know that something was the matter. My parents' rooms were at the opposite end of the house from our nursery, and on a different floor, and during the week we older children were away at school. Nonetheless, I'm sure it took all Mama's ingenuity to keep the household running, and at the same time shield us from our father's crises. Papa was "lying down for a little while," she told us. He would be "better soon." Absorbed in books, and in my own adventures, I didn't even think to inquire further.

My parents gave me a camera for my tenth birthday, and the first picture I took was of my father, standing by the river in his green wading boots. Looking at it now, I see the slight hunch of his back under the tweed jacket, the thin line of his rod curving off across the river. He seemed to me in those days to exist outside of time. But in fact he was not yet forty, younger than I am now.

Two years later, in 1968, my sister Isabella was born. Papa was well that year. I remember him leaning over her pram and taking photographs. I took more photographs myself, of James and Helena and John and our pet lamb, of Papa with his stick and small box camera, standing tall and stalwart in front of the house. We went to Greece that summer, renting a villa from Gavin's brother, Alymer. Papa sat by the water in a battered straw hat, delighting in the sun, the distant hills. He was a happy man.

That happiness lasted through the fall, and on into the Christmas holidays. Papa would appear in the Marchmont sitting room after a long day's shooting, smelling of gunpowder and sweat and *Eau Sauvage*, his cheeks still chilly from the frosty air. He'd be wearing his old tweed jacket and plus-fours, with the thick hand-knitted socks my mother had made. There was a sense of energy and competence: some mission well accomplished. Later that night, if there were visitors, he'd reappear in a tartan dinner jacket and bowtie. I'd watch him, warm and buoyant, pouring out the wine. He was the best father in the whole entire world.

4.

The older I grew, the more pleasure I took in Papa's company, not least because (unlike most other fathers) he was almost always to be found at home. In fact, *I* was the one who went away, first to boarding-school in Northumberland, and then down south to Sussex, where my mother had once gone. Back for the holidays, at eleven, twelve, thirteen, fourteen, the first thing I did was look for Papa. We sat in his study or in the library, talking, picking up again the endlessly tangled, endlessly fascinating conversation that went on between us. He would tell me all the home news, and I'd catch him up on what I had been reading or thinking about. I called him "GG" at this time, for "Generation Gap." He was, himself, the bridge across the chasm.

We spent much of our time together out of doors, fishing, shooting, going for walks. One summer morning, we got up at dawn and went out to shoot rabbits. I missed everything I fired at, but it didn't matter, we were both so much exhilarated by our time together: the mist rising from the hills, the greeny-gold grass in the early sun. Papa seemed especially moved by the familiar landscape. I remember him pausing to look back across a little valley. "Such a curiously beautiful view," he said aloud.

I was fourteen by then, and Papa forty-four, but such numbers meant very little. There was a certain deliberate innocence between us. It was as if we were asking each other over and over, *Are you a child, too? Are you a secret child?* Out in the woods or down by the burn, huddled together in the front seat of the car, we could invent for ourselves a safe, ungendered place, unmarked by differences in age or experience or strength. We could follow the track of our thoughts wherever they wanted to go.

I had a passion for guddling in those days, catching fish with my hands. A home movie exists from that same summer, of me guddling in the Swardon Burn: a flickering girlish face, long hair pulled back into a skinny pigtail. Papa's camera follows me as I wade downstream, feeling with my hands under the banks and into the deep crevices between the stones. At last I find a trout. There is a brief explosion as I grapple with it underwater and haul it up into the dry air. "Let's take a look," says Papa. And I hold it up for the camera, still in that flickering leafy light, bashful and proud.

At the time, I didn't catch the resonance of such a scene. I was enchanted by my father's company: filial, maternal, uncompromisingly loyal. It was as if I believed I never needed to grow up, would never have to grow into a sexual adult woman. And Papa encouraged me in this. I was his son, his acolyte, his page boy. In a parallel story, which was somehow just as true, I also felt completely free and genderless.

Meanwhile, my mother, weighed down by her own responsibilities, began to rely on me to keep an eye on Papa. He had never been especially interested in alcohol. But now he started to use it to console himself: one glass, then another. Soon, when Mama was away, I was the one who made sure he took his pills, or hustled him past friends who offered drinks. I was the one who sat with him at night while he watched television, or slowly turned the pages of his newspaper. We both did our best to pretend that nothing had changed. But the facts were obvious. I was a young girl growing into a young woman, a teenage daughter taking care of her troubled father. Papa saw this, even if I didn't. Skillfully, he played me against my mother. "All she talks about is God and gardening," he said. I had no idea how very old this new game was: *compare and contrast, divide and conquer.* I took what Papa said precisely at face value. I was proud and happy to be chosen as his confidante.

5.

Until the last year of my father's life (when I moved to California), I listened to his stories by the hour. He spoke most often about Marchmont, how lovely it was, and yet how impossible to keep going, how the boiler had broken down again, or the roof was leaking. Sometimes in a letter he'd concede, "I've been in bed for a week and have something wrong with me which I'm not sure about. V. boring." Or, "I have been rather ill and distracted lately by the prospects of all that may happen here." But when we talked together at home, there was never any mention made of illness. Both his highs and his lows felt like "truth" to him, his own necessary private weather. For the listener, however, they were two entirely different experiences.

Papa, manic, could be a difficult and demanding man, subject to sharp bursts of anger and impatience. At such times, the thwarted barrister would rise up in his full strength. One of his favorite tactics was to set up an argument with me on the opposing side and then proceed (in detail) to demolish it. The sheer drama of this enterprise was overwhelming. The air would be filled with his words, his hard-edged logic, his shiny accurate points, which for some reason I always imagined literally: rows and rows of them stretching off into the distance, like the gold paper-fasteners we used as knobs for our dolls' furniture. It was an extraordinary relief to get away.

The depressions were somewhat easier to deal with. Papa was more desolate perhaps, but also more generous and approachable. He could be touchingly appreciative of company. "*Darling*," he would say, making space beside him on the sofa. He relied on me, and to some extent on Katie and the younger children. But there was a judgment and an undertow here, too: Not everyone was welcome. "Who *are* these people?" he asked me once, staring down the length of the dining room table during some elaborate dinner party. And one summer I heard him bellowing at the parish priest, whom usually he thought of as an ally. "Go away," he kept shouting. "Go *away*! GO AWAY!"

Until I was fifteen, I had no way of making sense of any of this. I would have said that Papa was excited, or sometimes very sad, that maybe he had drunk too much the night before. But as far as I was concerned, there was nothing to be done about it. His different moods just had to be endured.

Then, early in 1972, after an especially difficult Christmas, my Aunt Clare took me aside and gave me the words to describe what Papa was going through, words like *clinic* and *lithium* and *manic depression* and, to me most crucially, *nervous breakdown*. Her own husband (Papa's brother, Jamie) had struggled with alcohol most of his life, and it may be she was weary of the endless subterfuge. I was grateful to be trusted in this way, but I was also frightened and confused. Jamie had died the previous year, swiftly followed by both of my beloved grandmothers. I was afraid that Papa would die, too. It didn't help that I was far away at boarding school, studying for my all-important O' levels. When I finally saw Papa again, I was taken aback by his appearance. His hair was so white, and he looked so old. "My heart sank about half a mile," I wrote in my journal.

I didn't learn the details till much later, but Papa was hospitalized twice that year, once in February (about the time I saw him) and once in May. Both times he was subjected to ECT. His illness had its pauses and relapses, but slowly, inexorably, he was getting worse. After Jamie died, he began. to drink more and more heavily. "He drank *suicidally*," said his brother, John Sebastian, remembering.

I still spent a lot of time with him during the holidays, and he still delighted in my enthusiasms and applauded my various achieve-ments at school. He gave me a pink suede jacket I adored. But there was a growing awkwardness between us, as I made the first faltering steps towards adult womanhood. "*Watch out*," he told me once. "You're just like me." I think it worried him to see this ardent younger self forced to negotiate the world from inside a woman's body, especially since I was not what he or any of his peers would have thought of as "desirable." When I looked at him now, I saw both love and judgment reflected in his eyes. He began to try, teasingly, but with a certain anxious insistence, to quiet me down. "Little velvet voice," he'd repeat mock-soothingly, or, quoting Lear after the death of Cordelia, "Her voice was ever soft/ Gentle and low, an excellent thing in a woman."

"Papa!" I'd protest, tossing my head impatiently. But I didn't forget the lines, or the sting of being muffled, thwarted, tamed.

I remember, too, driving with Papa when a report on menstrua-tion was announced on the radio. "We don't want to listen to *that*, do we?" Papa said, reaching for the knob. I was too shy to explain that I *did* want to listen to it, that in fact I was hungry for just such information. I wish now that we could have listened to it together, that we'd found a way to talk about these (to me) enormous changes, as we found a way to talk about so many other things. But Papa clicked the program off, and I did not protest. I knew, obscurely, that it was dangerous to emphasize my new femaleness. And because I loved the freedom that I'd had with Papa, as an androgyne, an honorary boy, I was ready to pretend puberty away if that was what he wanted. I had no wish to embarrass him, nor to be hauled forward into that uncomfortable new category of *woman,* where my mother reigned, and all my aunts and female cousins.

6.

By 1973, I was living in the family flat in London and studying for my A' levels. My parents appeared from Scotland now and then, and I talked to them often on the telephone. "Papa was very miserable indeed," I wrote in my journal that May. I wasn't doing especially well myself. My days seemed like a rug to me, "brightly striped with happiness and despair." There were "healthy red cuts on my inside left wrist from the latest razor play."

I described those cuts flippantly, but in fact I'd been "playing" at suicide for some time by then. I had made the first attempt at boarding school, overwhelmed by anxiety about Papa, and by my own impending exams. I took a number of sleeping pills and was preparing to take more. Luckily I was interrupted by a friend. "I won't try to kill myself again," I wrote in my journal.

But I did try again, at sixteen, seventeen, eighteen, nineteen–six or seven times in the course of the next five years. Some of those attempts were serious, others not. But none were unconnected, it strikes me now, with either puberty or my father.

I finished my A' levels towards the end of June, and Papa and I celebrated with a week-long trip to Morocco. Mama was very generous about letting us go off alone. I think she saw that we could both do with a break. We flew to Tangiers, then drove south over the narrow mountain roads to visit friends. My diary reminds me of the royal stables at Meknes, built to house 60,000 horses, and of a little valley near Chaouen, where egrets perched on a tree among the oleander and hibiscus. But our big discovery was Cap

Spartel, just ten miles from the center of Tangiers. Here the wild Atlantic roared around to join the warm and temperate Mediterranean. "The best swimming we had," I wrote, "great heat and deserted beaches, and huge pummeling waves."

Back in Tangiers, we lay by the hotel pool reading *Tess of the d'Urbervilles*, and went hunting for bargains in the *souk*, returning home laden with blue and green velvet carpets, and a white-painted bird cage for my aunt. We had one fabulous crisis where I quarreled with Papa, and he almost got arrested, chasing me across the dusky waste ground outside our hotel. It took time to convince the khaki-uniformed police that we did actually know each other: This man was my father, not some lecherous stranger. But for the most part we enjoyed ourselves enormously. "I haven't had such fun since Gavin died," said Papa.

7.

One of my father's minor interests was graphology, the ability to tell people's characters by their handwriting. Looking at my own adolescent script, which was round and clear and almost completely lacking in tops and tails, he proclaimed me "greedy-for-life." And it was true. As he himself grew sadder and more reclusive, refusing social invitations, hiding out from unexpected visitors, I seized each chance to reach out and explore. The following spring, I took off for Thailand, working for three months at a Catholic leprosy mission, traveling into the jungle to give out soap and baby food and vitamins. I wrote quantities of letters while I was away, and kept a voluminous journal. On return, I wrote up my experiences in a colored scrapbook, illustrated with my own photographs. I gave it to Papa to read when I was finished, and he wrote to me appreciatively, "Whatever you do, you have a formidable and never-to-be-neglected weapon or defence or help in your true ability to write."

It wasn't characteristic of him to give praise so directly, and I hardly dared let myself accept it. But the sentence stayed with me, nonetheless. No one had asked me to put together that scrapbook. But doing it had felt crucial, with that internal insistence I would later come to trust. It mattered that Papa should have blessed the enterprise.

Meanwhile, he had fallen into another slump, and was treated once again with ECT. As so often, he refused to take his pills, turning instead to alcohol in a vain effort at self-medication. My diary tracks the hidden bottles, the ugly battles with my mother, the cruel side-cuts at me and the younger children. For months, I kept on listening, trying to cope. But when I brought my first boyfriend home to visit, and he stayed up late with Papa, drinking; when he blundered into my room to kiss me with Papa's liquor on his breath; then, at last, I started to get angry. My father was a sick man, this I understood. But that sickness had its consequences, and not only for himself.

"First you love them," wrote Oscar Wilde. "Then you judge them. Sometimes, you forgive them." I loved Papa, but I had begun to judge him, too. His misery was overwhelming. And I was weary with the endless arguments, the rages and the righteousness, the scorn. There was a series of accidents, too, around this time: car crashes, unexpected falls. I remember a broken nose and two black eyes, a patched wrist, something wrong with his elbow. My father was not yet fifty, but he had begun to look like an old man. His hair and sideburns were turning white, and his face was red and swollen, with a strange, corrugated surface. I wanted to scoop him up and carry him off and save him, and at the same time I wanted someone else to do it. I felt imprisoned by his neediness, his long nostalgic tales. In self protection, I began to take notes, to write down his broken phrases as I helped put him into bed. Inevitably, he saw what I was up to. "You can put me in a novel," he told me once.

In 1975, after my first year at Cambridge, I went back to the Far East. Papa tried to persuade me not to go. *"Please* not Laos." The US forces had just left, and he was sure it was about to become a puppet state, "just like South Vietnam, Cambodia, and probably Thailand."

I was alarmed by these warnings, but I went anyway, traveling by bus from Khon Kaen to Nong Khai, and on across the Mekong River to Vientiane. It was a strange time to visit. The Pathet Lao (Communists) had been fighting the Royal Army for a year, and many foreigners had already left. I spent my days with an old French nun, Soeur Jeanne Thérèse, following her around the boarded-up city, from the tuberculosis ward to the ward for indigents, and on to numerous private houses, distributing medicine and clothes. At night I slept in the Convent of Dara Samuth, which had once housed 800 students. Now the grass grew long and unkempt, and the nuns were living on rice and vegetables and home-made yoghurt. If I refused some treat, they urged me to reconsider: "You mustn't leave it for the Pathet!"

In the years that followed, I took to the road at every opportunity, hitching across Ireland and France and Holland, exploring London with friends, traveling alone (by Greyhound bus) around the United States. Despite his own reclusiveness, Papa did his best to encourage me. "I am all for the exhilarating capital of the world, enlarged by M.C.," he wrote to me in New York City. "Don't get mugged."

8.

I returned from America in the summer of 1977. For a week that August, the whole family went up to Skye. My father had just come back from the ninth (and last) of his ECT treatments, but Mama was the only one who knew of this. She kept explaining that Papa was "treading water" (a curious phrase, it strikes me now). The rest of us were appalled. Papa looked much thinner, and his hair was sparse and tangled. When I asked what he was thinking about, he answered, "Death."

"He's *awful*," my sister Katie said.

His depression continued through the fall, and on into the new year. Home for Christmas, I listened to him by the hour. "Long talk Papa," says my tiny pocket diary. "Talking to Papa for a very long time."

These "talks" were mostly desolate one-liners, breathed out in whispers as I helped him into bed or sat beside him at a crowded dinner table. He was not speaking to me exactly, but to the person I'd become in fifteen, twenty years. It was as if he felt himself to be already dead. "I was so happy," he said, "and now it's *revolting*." And then of Mama, "She bears the terrible brunt."

When I tried to tell him there were good times still to come, he answered carefully, "There are for you," and then, with great intensity, "You live your *own* life."

He had always claimed that there was nothing wrong with him, "nothing that half a million pounds wouldn't cure." But by the following Easter he wasn't pretending anymore. "I'm not all right," he told me. "I'm drunk all the time. Lucian [Kate's lover] knows I'm not all right."

He had grown yet thinner and more pimply. He now said outright that he was dead, had been dead a long time. "I *used* to love my children," he said mournfully. "You still do, Papa," I tried to reassure him. But he refused to take it in. "I'd like to live on an island," he said, "and drink myself to death."

Untreated manic depression runs a savage course, growing only worse with each recurrence. Alcoholism has a similar trajectory. In the last years of his life, my father was immobilized by both. He spent time in various hospitals and detox centers, but none had any lasting effect. He had entered what my mother referred to as "the dark night."

She, meanwhile, was working hard to keep afloat, torn between Papa, her charity commitments and her six tall children, all between the ages of ten and twenty-two. Papa professed great admiration for her energy and dedication, but he didn't have much empathy for her. "I ought to have married you," he told me. "At least you'd shout at me and throw me around. I thought I *was* marrying you, really."

He wrote a series of short stories around that time, wrestling with the problem of good and evil, and he spoke to me endlessly of Marchmont. "I hate it. I hate it. And I love it far too much." He was being "un-buried," he said, brought back from drowning. I sat next to him, listening in my head to Ariel's song from *The Tempest*, and shifting the pronouns to suit.

> *Full fathom five my father lies,*
> *Of his bones are coral made;*
> *Those are pearls that were his eyes . . .*

He was a great silver salmon, its flesh rotting, its scales tarnished and worn. It seemed impossible to haul him up from under water.

9.

Soon after I got back from that first visit to America, I had a dream. "What shall I *do?*" I asked a friend. A crowd of people answered me in chorus, "*Everything that is different,*" they said. Someone brought me soup and sat me down to eat. Someone else offered to teach me how to drive. Making plans would only hold me back, they told me. I had to follow paths I had not yet found.

It was clear to me by then that this was true. Papa might believe that I was still "greedy-for-life," but in fact I had been struggling for quite some time. He was not the only one who was contemplating suicide.

"If there were a building to jump off, and I would not be saved, mangled, put together again, I would jump off . . . I am ready to be dead-ed, as it were."

Other friends at Cambridge felt as I did. But it wasn't just work that made me desperate, or the highly competitive social scene, or the fact that in my day at least, men outnumbered women nine to one. Cambridge was stressful and demanding, yes. But Papa was still my overriding concern. I'd been encouraged all my life to think that he'd "be better soon," and meanwhile he was only getting worse. It was hard not to take the blame for failing him. I was afraid, too, not just for him, but for myself. *Watch out*, Papa had always said. *You're just like me.* I began to wonder if he weren't right, after all.

What did it mean to be "the same" as Papa? Would I spend my days huddled in front of the television with the sound turned off? Would I turn mad and sad and drink too much? No one mentioned genetic predisposition. But I did know that my paternal grandfather and great grandfather had both been subject to depression, as had my grandmother on my mother's side. And with two of Papa's brothers dead before the age of fifty, there was no mistaking the power of alcohol in the family. I did not yet possess all the different pieces of this puzzle (I'd never heard of Alcoholics Anonymous, for example, or Al-Anon, or ACOA), but I did take what action I could. I stopped drinking quite suddenly when I was sixteen. And though I experimented with drugs at Cambridge (everything from heroin to mescaline to cannabis to acid), I was fiercely determined not to become an addict.

I was equally wary of abandoning my life and turning into Papa's perfect nurse. For years I'd seen my mother as "ordinary" in comparison to my seductively melancholy, *interesting* father. Now I seemed boring and predictable myself, at least to my sister Katie and her friends. They taunted me for my earnestness and made fun of me behind my back, egged on by Lucian. I had no idea what to do. How be "cool" and witty, and at the same time satisfy my father's growing needs? How put in all the hours of necessary study? How make a self I could inhabit and enjoy?

It would take me years to come up with answers to these questions. In the meantime, lost and floundering, perhaps I was guided by that chorus of dream voices. *Do everything that is different*, they had told me. Early in 1979, I applied for a Fulbright scholarship to the United States.

10.

I worked hard at Cambridge that last year, writing two dissertations, both of which required massive amounts of original research. I was hoping to get a First, as my father had done. Instead, I collapsed in my final exams, which coincided horribly with the first few days of my period. I had foreseen that this was likely to happen, and had tried to explain my problem to the authorities. But they refused to take me seriously. The exams had to take place on the appointed dates, they told me. There was no precedent for changing the rules. I left the exam room in floods of tears, deeply humiliated by this display of female frailty.

Later, back home, I tried to talk about it with my mother. But Papa kept interrupting. Was he embarrassed by the subject, or did he simply want *himself* to be the focus of attention? I don't know the answer. But something broke in me at his insistence. For years I'd listened to him, put him first. Now I wanted solace, and he wouldn't give it, wouldn't even let my mother give it. I was furious and unforgiving. I still remember Mama driving us to Edinburgh in the crowded Mini, he, as always, set on making some important point, while I stared blindly out the window, refusing with all my heart to pay attention.

Despite the giant letdown of my finals, I did win that Fulbright scholarship to Berkeley, and in August 1979, flew out to California to get settled. I found a communal house on the Berkeley/Oakland border, with five lively housemates, and a fruit tree in the garden. "I hope that Berkeley turns out all that you have hoped for," Papa wrote, "and that it will lead to a far better and more useful life than at least one of your relations."

Berkeley seemed gentle and generous, and, a new word, "mellow." I liked my professors and the work I was doing. But as the months passed, the missives from home grew increasingly grim. Papa spent whole pages fretting about the state of the world. "I wish you were here and I could talk to you," he wrote. And, "I wish I were back in Morocco with you, in those waves, with *Eau Sauvage*."

I was happy to remember Morocco and the "wild water" at Cap Spartel. But other, less easy memories rose up, too: Papa sitting on the sofa one Christmas, his trouser legs hitched up, his glasses smeared; Papa red and spotty and miserable, lying on the grass at Cambridge, his sad head resting on his upper arm. And there were the words, too, echoing down the years, words of desperation, words of encouragement:

> *You're better than me. Mentally, we're the same person.*
> *We're very alike–terrifyingly alike. So watch out!*
> *Grasp what you want, that's the thing. Just do what you want.*
> *Don't do what I do, do what I say. Go your own way.*
> *Perhaps you aren't old enough to understand. You've so much life in front of you. I did try to tell you.*

In April 1980, I turned twenty-four. My family rang me from Scotland to wish me happy birthday. The connection was good, and Papa's voice sounded close in my ear. "You sound as if you are in *Greenlaw*," he marveled, naming the local village. There was a pause, and then he added, slyly, truthfully, "Some of us miss you more than others."

Papa died of a heart attack early on that tumultuous Sunday, the day Mount St. Helens blew up. He was sitting at home in the tiny washroom outside the library, looking at photographs from a book called *The Best of Life*. The previous day, he'd gathered armfuls of sweet-smelling pheasant's eye, a very beautiful white narcissus, with a sharp reddish-orange center. The flowers survived to scent the chapel at his funeral.

The day he died, I'd been scheduled to work at a feminist bookstore in San Francisco, and the news so bewildered me that I took the BART train in as usual. "Did you like him?" my boss asked casually, when I explained what had happened. "Were you close?"

I was too shaken to serve customers that day, so some other task was given to me: filing order slips, I think it was. *Did I like him?* The question seemed absurd. My beloved mountain had been blown sky high. Spirit Lake was clogged. Rivers of mud were racing down into the plains. *Had we been close?* This man was my emperor, my audience, my whole applause. I couldn't begin to imagine what life would be without him.

At Mount St. Helens now, eighteen years after the explosion, the ravaged landscape is beginning to recover. Among the first flowers to return was pearly everlasting, which, curiously enough, is used for funeral wreaths. Fireweed came back, too, within three months, along with lupine and groundsel and thistle, and these weeds gradually formed the basis for more complex growth, including pasqueflower, huckleberries, and Indian paintbrush. Coyotes have been seen again, feasting on wild strawberries. Spirit Lake, much wider now, and higher by some 200 feet, once more reflects the blue light of the sky.

For months and years after Papa died, I remained seared and shaken by his absence. He was only fifty-three. It seemed to me outrageous that other people's fathers should still be alive, at sixty-three, seventy-three, eighty-three, while Mama and the rest of us had to shoulder on alone. I missed his praise, his fierce, exultant watching. At the same time, I did not allow myself to forget what a weighty responsibility he had sometimes been. In a dream which still seems to me crucial, he came to me naked, asking for help and shelter. He was Lear on the storm-blasted heath, and I a latter-day Cordelia, trying to hold to my own truth in the face of his devouring need. "I'll give you anything you want," I told him. "But not my soul-stuff. You've got to find another coat to cover you." It was the sort of thing I never could have said in the old days, when the darling one, the old devourer, always managed to get his way, no matter what. Even now, I marvel at that dream. It was far wiser than I was myself.

Years passed, and I came out as a lesbian. I read *On Lies, Secrets, and Silence* by Adrienne Rich, *Sister Outsider* by Audre Lorde, and (because I worked at the feminist press, Virago) armfuls of women's poetry and novels. This reading schooled me, taught me to unpack the mixed blessings of my inheritance, and to look,

clear-eyed, at my beloved father. Slowly I began to see what a
confusing figure he had sometimes been: in his maleness, his
misery, his manic overwhelm. "I think of Papa luxuriating in his
despair," wrote my brother James, years later. "And I thank him
for his lessons."

James is dead now, a suicide at twenty-two. He'd been taking
heroin, but it may be that he also suffered, as does my brother
John, from bipolar manic depression. Men and women are equally
subject to this, though in my family it seems to occur more
frequently among the adult men. I have moods and melancholies of
my own, but I no longer believe that I'm *just like* my father. In
the years since his death, I have been free to come up with other
role models: women writers and artists and activists, the occasional
sane, sweet-tempered man. Through them, and through my friend-
ships, I have gradually begun to inhabit my life more fully, and in
the process, to recover some of the humor and exuberance I lost
as a young girl. I had a second (lesbian) adolescence in my late
twenties and early thirties, where for the first time I experienced
myself as "good-looking": a lean, tomboyish character with a mop
of dark hair, and the big greeny-gray eyes I had inherited. "See,
Papa!" I wanted to shout up to him in heaven. "You needn't have
worried. Some people think I'm all right, after all!"

The McEwen family crest is *Reviresco*: "I grow again." It shows
a blasted oak, with new shoots springing from the torn and
battered trunk. My world was blown sky-high the day my father
died, and I sometimes think that I'm still picking up the pieces. But
the roots I've put down since are real, too. The woman I live with
now is more like Papa, in her restless argumentative brain and her
tender, complex heart, than anyone else I've met along the way. It
is perhaps not coincidental that she is also a sober alcoholic, with
a difficult history of her own. We have a shabby, comfortable
country life together, filled with books and cats and hard work and
conversation.

Meanwhile my father's voice still occupies my head. I own his
Chekhov and his Rilke now, his dark red cashmere jersey. A

watercolor of his hangs on the wall. Last year, I spent a few days with my mother and my youngest sister on the Scottish island of Iona. As we walked together through the nunnery gardens, bird song erupted from a distant tree. I ran over to find out what it was and caught sight of a robin red-breast laying claim to its territory. I'd never heard such a racket from so small a bird. "Hello, Papa," I called to it in passing. And then I hurried back to join the others.

The Trouble with Horses

Carol Potter

He had arms he couldn't
understand.

His arms were horses
with bits clamped between their teeth,

two horses bolting, a pack of children
clinging to their backs,

fifty child fingers
digging in the horses' manes.

The manes blew
in the children's faces,

their faces were balloons
rising from their necks,

their necks were saplings
rising from their bodies.

Surprised to find so much air,
already the children were trying to forgive.

152

The Trouble with Boats

Carol Potter

The children were stones in the boat.
They knew they had promised to sit

quietly with their hands folded in their laps,
but they kept shifting side to side between

their grown-ups, threatening to tip them all.
One grown-up said, "I don't know how to swim,"

and the other one kept saying, "It's too hard
to row with such un-predictable weight rolling

at the bottom." The children were trying to sing,
not knowing how hard it could be

to sing
without opening their mouths.

Because There Was Nothing to Do with the Hands

Carol Potter

When the cattle buyer drove off up the road yelling,
"See you later, alligators," and my brothers and I
hollered back, "In a while, crocodile!" our father told us
it was impolite, we should settle down. He told us
we should take care.
That summer, everywhere we went, we stood staring
at whatever there was to stare at with our feet apart,
our hands resting at the tops of our heads, our fingers
interlocked because we didn't know what to do with our hands.
We stood like that under the apple tree in August
watching slug after slug hit the cow's skull,
each bullet hole opening like a flower
between her eyes while she stood staring back
at our father
and refusing to fall.
He had a German Luger in his hand, the gun
captured at Buchenwald. He had taken pictures, he said,
because he knew no one would believe
what he'd seen. That summer, digging
through the hall closet, I found
those pictures, bodies
one on top of the other, stripped—
everything gone, heart, flesh, soul, gone out—
hands lying beside the bodies
like loose clothes.
My father couldn't explain it.
In one picture people stand at a fence—

eyes wide open, fingers
tight on the wire.
It was from that camp the gun came.
My brothers and I stood watching
with our hands cupped at the tops of our heads
because there was nothing to do with the hands.
Because it was too hot to bury them in pockets.

Earbobs

Minnie Bruce Pratt

We've finished midday dinner at my mother's house, me and my youngest son on holiday from college. Mama goes down the hall to her bedroom and brings back a fake leather jewelry box, which she sets on the formica kitchen table. She's taken out the pieces she still wears; I can have anything I want of what's left. My boy and I rummage in the necklaces, pins, earrings. Here is *Mother* spelled out in fake pearls; I don't remember that she ever pinned it on. Here are the pink pearl screw-on earbobs, older than me, nubbly as nipples; she wore those with her tailored rose-pink suit. Such tiny earrings for such a big woman. Nowadays she says to me, "I wear clothes that most women wouldn't." She means her extra-large sturdy men's nightshirts, her sensible shoes.

But she always dressed me like a girl, knitted my sweaters, sewed all my clothes. My favorite dress was dark blue taffeta with black braid. I wore it the winter I started menstruating; my skin glided under the silky taffeta. She made the blue-flowered voile with a white collar that I wore the spring I got engaged. She made my wedding dress, white velvet, and the black velvet dress suit I wore home to my bridal shower. She was mad I'd put it on before I was married; I didn't understand that black was for after the ceremony. She sent clothes when I was married to my first husband, his and hers jeans jackets, but I bought the yellow polka-dot chiffon maternity dress that lasted through two pregnancies. After I left him and began living as a lesbian, her presents one holiday were a pair of white pearl earrings and a plaid flannel jacket.

* * *

156

When my father died, she took me to their room, to his closet, and asked if I wanted any of his clothes. She expected me to want something. I chose a white cotton dress shirt, a thin black-and-red striped tie, and his summer panama hat. Later that year, when I did poetry readings in the South, I wore his clothes. When women asked me what the hat meant, I said it made me feel powerful. Was I cross-dressing as my father, for my mother? I thought I was becoming a lesbian . . .

Pa

Minnie Bruce Pratt

On my way to supper with a friend, to gossip about love affairs, mine and hers, I put the photographs of you in my bag, the black-and-white ones taken in San Francisco. You squat in front of a graffiti wall in your grey suit, elegant nonchalance against the dirt. You stand in the dappled sunshine and the weeds with your jacket slung over your shoulder like a film noir movie star. I gloat over the pictures, and then pause to clear a few more pieces of debris from my desk. I sift through the mess of papers, turning up another photograph, my father and mother soon after they were married. She stands like a schoolgirl, feet primly together, hands behind her back, but this time the one I see is my father. They are side by side, but he does not touch her. His eyes are cautious under his fedora. In his double-breasted suit, cigarette in hand, he is a man of the world, debonair. I meet his eyes, and my heart shuts and opens under my breastbone as if you had come up behind me and slid your hands around my waist.

The last time he touched me without thinking first, he held my hand, I was three or four, and I was his. He tipped his panama hat to everyone he met as they admired his baby, too young to be a girl, who twirled on the lunch counter stool while his buddies fed her ice cream. He carried her across the shining river on his back. On the muddy bank he yelled, "Hold 'em," as she jerked spiny invisible catfish out with a cane pole. He said, "Jump like me, run like me," and when she couldn't, he walked away. Her mama said to a neighbor, "He did want a boy." In his rocking chair, he watched Friday night boxing, Saturday afternoon baseball. He

158

watched the boys he had once been write their names in the air with fists and arms. He rocked, he drank beer, whiskey, moonshine, he rocked and cried. At the funeral home, his best friend sat in her white oxford shirt and her brown polyester slacks. She sat with her knees spread wide apart and chain-smoked Camels, like him. She told the story of how, many years ago, he would not go to see the brother he loved most in the world be married. She pressed two fingers tight together. "He loved him like this, like this," she said, her fingers lying as close together as lovers.

The second time I met you, I wondered if we would be lovers. In a theatrical foyer crowded with dressed-up lesbians, you were wearing your grey suit. You were armored, aloof. I wanted to put my hand on your arm, but I thought you were saying, "No." Yet later, by myself in the night, I closed my eyes and returned to you, wordlessly, and without a word you gathered me into your arms. You sent a black-and-white postcard, an ambiguous figure in trenchcoat, pants, heavy shoes, striding through the steam of a manhole cover, rising up from the underground. If I had sent you a photograph of myself then, it would have been the white flowers of jimsonweed, almost angel trumpets, open at dusk in a waste place, against the cement rubble of a city block, or on limestone rocks jumbled by the river.

You told me, over and over, that you wanted me to be your girl. Now sometimes you call me your femme, or you say, "You are so smart, that's why I call you girl." Sometimes I hold you, brushing my hand over the silky stubble of your hair, and say, "You're my girl, you're my boy." Now when we lie together you hold me and infinitesimally rock me, rock me, caught in the backwash of the river. Not my mama nor my pa ever rocked me this way, timeless, the little waves lapping at the muddy bank, leaving a thin script, a tender mark on the skin of dirt.

Just Like Him

Laura Markowitz

My father is strong and wide, a raft to cling to in unpredictable waters. I came from the depths of my mother, but I'm tethered to my father by something beyond this body's beginning. When I lean on him, I hear his heart beating steady and my universe curves back to its starting place.

I want to be a woman like my mother: outspoken, joyful, ready to laugh. I want to be a man like my father: gentle, generous, in control. For the first half of my life, I believed my father was invulnerable. I thought if I was just like him, I would never feel sadness, anger, fear. I wanted to wear my skin the way he wore his, wrapped in a wall of muscle through which nothing could hurt. I thought I could escape the fate of my mother, who was sickly, who was weak, who died. I relied on him to be infallible. He never raged at us kids when we grew wild in our silliness or squabbles. He never complained when he found himself with three angry teenagers to raise and a dying wife to grieve. He never said, "Me first" to any of us. Never, not even now, not yet.

I knew my dad better than most of my friends knew theirs because he chose not to be a commuter father, foregoing the prestigious law firms of Manhattan for a modest office of his own nine minutes away. Every few months, for no special reason, he would take a day off from work to take my sister, brother or me into the city to see a play, or go to the circus, or wander around the zoo. Dressed in my party clothes, I held onto his warm hand as he steered me into the grown-up world. My office is seven minutes from my house. I take a day off every so often to wander through the park or climb the rocks by the river, because he taught me that time rushes us along and we have to remember what matters.

My father once told me about my childhood, "I loved you like a mother." I know what he means, the kind of love that makes your heart grow so wide you wonder that it doesn't split right open and spill itself out. It's the love that never says, "Me first." During my adolescence, when I was so bottled up inside after my mother died, he couldn't say words out loud to comfort me, because he was treading water in his own numb ocean. But his heart was whispering love to mine, upholding me as best he could. Like the time he took me to Yankee Stadium and five minutes after we sat down, I felt like I would explode if I didn't get right home, and I couldn't say why. He just took my hand and said, "Whatever you want, honey. Let's go."

My father and I are so close it hurts. When we say goodbye, he says, "I love you," as if it might be the last chance he will ever have to tell me this. As I back the car out of his driveway, we both wave until we are out of each other's sight. The long drive home always begins with dread in the pit of my stomach. I curse myself for living so far away. What's the point of sharing this lifetime if we rarely get to see each other? I brood on this until we cross the George Washington Bridge and enter the wasteland of the New Jersey Turnpike. Only with the Hudson River between us do I start to breathe normally again. When I get home, I call and let him know I arrived safely. Then, I feel my thirty-four years fit back on me again and my own life enfolds me with a pleasurable relief. It might be weeks before we speak on the phone, and when we do it feels sweet and real, not of epic proportions.

I come from parents who stayed in love with each other for their entire marriage, and so I grew up believing I, too, would be in love with someone forever. I listened to the story of how my father and mother met in 1958, all the while picturing myself meeting the stranger who would become my fate. He was just out of law school and serving in the Army. On leave in Chicago, he was to meet up with his cousin's college friend–my mom–who was in graduate school at the time. But she already had plans to be out of town with her boyfriend. She generously offered my father her apartment while she was away. She left him a key and a note that said, "Make yourself at home." He went to sleep in her bed.

She unexpectedly came home that night, late, having broken up with the boyfriend. She forgot he was there. My dad was asleep. She screamed when she found him, a strange man in her bed. For years, I confused this story with *Goldilocks and the Three Bears*.

Soon after they met, my father was stationed in Germany and my mother came for a holiday. They took off on a tour of Europe in his VW Beetle. I used to imagine him singing "You Are My Sunshine" to her, slow-paced and slightly off key, the same way he sang to us in the car. He was late in returning to the base because the car had broken down. That one day stuck in Italy was significant–his whole unit was shipped off to Beirut without him. We were sure it was a sign that he was destined to come back home, marry my mom and have us kids.

My father believes we have a psychic connection. "You always say just what I was thinking," he tells me. Maybe it's true, or maybe I have spent my entire life studying him, copying him, absorbing his stories into me, making them mine. Secretly, I think that daughters are supposed to want to be like their mothers, but much as I loved and clung to my mother, it was into my father's image I wanted to mold myself.

As a girl, I wanted to be just like him. I studied him each morning as he adjusted his tie, the way he lifted his chin, the corners of his mouth turned down as he tugged the knot into place. After the tie was straightened, I listened for the snap of his watchband. I wanted one just like his, even though the clasp pinched me once, because it seemed much more advanced than simply an instrument to measure the passage of the sun. I studied the hieroglyphics on the outer rim, orbiting the glow-in-the-dark numbers on the face. I imagined my father lost in Iceland using his watch as a map to the sea. I imagined him holding his watch to his ear and hearing the pulse of a volcano about to erupt. My mother's watch was a woman's watch–small, dainty and only good for measuring how late we were in the morning, or what time we had to go to bed, or if he was on his way home from work. I wanted a man's life, an explorer's life, not a woman's life of waiting and worrying. My watch had a picture of Winnie the Pooh with one hand in the honey jar and another holding a red balloon.

What I wanted to inherit from my father was his certainty. He was so sure he could protect the ones he loved, even though nothing in life is certain. In the first grade, the television full of Patty Hearst, I was afraid of being kidnapped. If my parents were leaving us with a babysitter, I would lie in bed miserable with grim fantasies. Before they left, my father would sit on the edge of my bed and assure me: "This is my castle. No one can come in here and hurt you. I wouldn't let them." Already, at age six, I knew he wanted it to be true, but that the truth was there were no guarantees.

Last week, on the telephone, I told him, "I won't have children. I worry sometimes that I'll be all alone when I'm old." He answered with that same, familiar certainty, "No, you won't be." For a whole hour, I believed him, netted by his voice of authority, his absolute power to know these things. Is it the wishful thinking of a man unwilling to accept that he can't control the winds and the storms that assail the people he loves? Or is it the prayer of a man who believes he can sway the universe to his will if his heart is pure?

While my father and I have always been close, he could not understand me when I tried to explain why it was frustrating to be a girl, what I was up against. In the car on the way to school, he would discuss my school subjects with me and talk about cases he was working on–the landlord who wouldn't replace the air conditioning, the tenant who refused to pay his rent. I was studying Talmud in my Jewish Day School and told him what the rabbis said about what you should do if you find money, if someone harms you, if your bull wanders into the neighbor's pasture. He took me seriously, and so I took myself seriously. But I complained about having to wear a dress every Friday, Shabbat, which all the girls had to do. He didn't grasp the politics of it–how the boys, in their pants, took over the playground and lorded it over us; how we girls, in our dresses and party shoes, could not run, could not climb or tackle. We clustered together playing monotonous games of cat's cradle. My father didn't understand the constant expectation to be sweet, pretty, soft-spoken, mother's little helper. He could only say, "But you look so pretty in a dress!" I wished for a suit jacket like his, with the inside pocket perfect for secrets and a satin lining like another skin warm against my arms. He patted my hand and told me the same thing my aunts told me, "Someday, when you grow up, you'll be interested in dresses."

They were wrong about that. My coming out as a lesbian seemed to explain my resistance and gave me permission to hate the strangling dress code of femininity. Now my father saves me his old shirts, worn in at the cuffs, oversized and running down to my knees. I wrap up in them when I have a cold or when I feel more fragile than usual, as if wearing my father's armor can still protect me from what is frightening.

I don't know what my father and I would be to each other if my mother had lived. In 1975, a year when so many of my friends' parents were divorcing, my father drove every evening to the Bronx to visit his wife in the hospital. Lying in bed, I would hear him come back at night, the distinct creak as he climbed the stairs. He would pause in front of my door before he flipped off the hall light switch and went into his own room, always leaving his door open a crack so we knew we could wake him up anytime, no matter what. With the logic of a teenager, I wanted him to come in and talk to me, and was angry when he didn't, yet on the rare occasion when he would come in, I was equally furious with him and barely said a word.

My mother wrote me a last letter before she died, telling me how proud she was that I was becoming just like my father. I imagine that this also worried her because she saw me following his example, closing in around my confusion and pain. She encouraged me to talk about my feelings during her illness, but I resisted, rolled my eyes. For many years after she died, I was grateful to my father for the safe retreat of silence, but it was also a terrible trap. Being alike, we could not comfort each other, could not grieve together. At the same time, he had become transparent to me, and I saw him, with some shock, as a flawed human being. His mournful presence became suffocating. The way he said my name, the sound of him chewing, the way he hummed tunelessly to the radio, became unbearable. I saw all his faults, hated him for having them, hated that my mother had died, resented that her death made my father so sad.

It was around that time that I began preparing to become an orphan. I expected the car crash, the mugger, the heart attack as I stood waiting for him to come home from work. My nose pressed against the glass panes of the front door, the smell of cold glass metallic like the taste of blood, I scratched his name in the cloud of my breath and raged at him for abandoning me, even though he was the one who lived. When the car finally swung into the driveway, I fled to my room.

Years later, I am still waiting to be left. I imagine what it will be like to become a widow; I wake up at night next to her and rehearse what it will feel like not to have her long, smooth body stretched out across the bed when the summer air floods the room with sweet grass and cricket hum. I wonder if I will be like him, stoic in my grief, loyal to the dead with an unwavering heart.

*   *   *

In my early twenties, home for a memorial service for my father's uncle Jack, I asked my dad, "What do you think happens when we die?" I wanted to sound casual, a trick he taught me when asking something important, to reassure the other person that it's safe to answer honestly. He said, "I think that's it. That's the end. We have one life, we live it, and then it's over." I thought about my mother. Was she really gone? Not watching from a cloud, not waiting and judging us from some perch, not feeling hurt because we love other people now?

At some point when I was in high school, my father announced to me that he had an evening "appointment." My friends and I were in the basement listening to music when he returned to the house with a woman in bright orange lipstick–his "appointment." He had forgotten their theater tickets. Embarrassed, we never spoke about it, and I never saw the woman again.

After his dating was out of the closet, I tried to ignore it. Then he started to spend more time with Neala, someone he had known for years. She had two young children and was divorcing. I was not interested in being a big, happy family with them. I wanted to survive high school and get away to college. One year, he invited Neala and her children over for dinner for Mother's Day and insisted I come downstairs and eat with them. I felt betrayed by his disloyalty to my mother and to me. I stormed away from the table and, when he didn't come after me, I cried alone in my room and counted the days until I could leave.

A year after I left home to go to college, Neala and her children moved into my father's house. At the kitchen table with him on a rare visit home, I listened as he told me in halting language how he realized he loved her and wanted to be with her. I was completely embarrassed by this revelation of my father as someone who was so emotional. I was also immensely relieved that he might now be happy again.

I grew to love Neala, a kind woman with a generous heart. Over the years, our whole family has grown close. Our strongest bond is that we all love him and laugh at his foibles. We gang up on him and tell him, "Stop futzing around!" when we're late and trying to leave the house and he is wandering off to change a light bulb.

As long as my father lives, I am still somebody's child. Whether I want to or not, I look to him to teach me how to grow older, how to be an adult and think about money, work, family, love. I suspect one day he will teach me how to die. After all the obsessive thought I've given to this matter, I still can't imagine how the planet will keep spinning on that day. I hold onto the hope that this lifetime isn't all there will be for us. It seems inconceivable that we arrive here, love one another and then flicker out and it's all over. I like to imagine myself leaning into his heartbeat for a thousand-thousand lifetimes, with my mother, my sister and brother, their children, my beloved, Neala, her children, all surrounding him as we surround each other. I marvel at the mysterious ties more enduring than our accumulated breaths.

Victoria Told Me Her Secret

Debbra Palmer

My father is suspicious of my wardrobe.
Guilty, my thick-soled shoes–
a militant line
at the bottom of my closet.

Practical shirts
with mannish collars and tails
swing on plastic hangers
above the shoes.

Across a rack of denim
or khaki trousers,
a row of brimmed caps,
and nearby an unflattering
red and black checkered robe.

He never says so, but I suspect
my father thinks
that I have a false bottom in my chest of drawers
where I store
my dominatrix suit, my whip,
and sculpted silicone items.

During a long-distance conversation
he compares me to videos
he has seen
of two or more women
moaning and rolling
like cats in heat

168

tonguing the air
pretending to hurt
or to please each other.

He admits that many men
share this fantasy.

While he expounds on this
my body turns plastic and
welds to the phone.

I wish he were here in person
so I could deck him
right out of his shoes.
I'd pull out the lifts
he walks on to look taller than
hot pink California girls
and force him to wear his new wife's lingerie
that cuts and scratches
the genitals.

I would pull out his stash of sex toys
and line them up like bowling trophies.

I'd send him running
from his own secrets
but he'd find
that wearing stilettos impedes him,
and the secrets
catch up,
tackle,
and deep kiss him
red hair and lipstick everywhere,
ramming their tongues down his throat
just the way he
doesn't
like it.

Fishergirl

Gretchen Legler

I am speeding across Nebraska on a train, on my way to Salt Lake City from St. Paul to meet my mother. We are going to travel the "Anasazi Circle," driving through Utah, Colorado, New Mexico and Arizona to see the ruins of ancient pueblos–Hovenweep, Chaco Canyon, Canyon de Chelly and Mesa Verde. Early in our planning my mother told me that my father would not be able to accompany us because he would not have time off. "You know," I said to her, "this is just for us. Me and you." She said she knew that from the start, but that she didn't want to put it that way to him. "Maybe you'll go on a trip like this with him someday," she said.

It saddens me that I can hardly imagine my father and me in a car together, traveling the West, staying in hotels, eating at roadside cafes, sharing small details of our lives. The only thing we have ever done together is fish. Fishing is the way we have known each other, and slenderly, silently, even then. When we fish, I am Fishergirl, still eighteen and living at home, and he is my fishing father. Beyond these stories we have written for ourselves, beyond these stories we have written for and on each other, the rest of who we are seems to fall tragically away.

There is a picture of me, taken by my brother Austin, in which I am dressed up as a fly fisher. I am eighteen years old, and I am on my first fly-fishing trip to Yellowstone National Park. I stand in the woods, a stream behind me, a pair of heavy waders strapped over each shoulder, baggy at the hips and waist. My plaid shirt sleeves are rolled up, my tanned arms bare to the elbow. My fishing vest is hung with gadgets. A piece of fleece on one shoulder is decorated with half a dozen flies. On my head is a gray felt hat, a goose feather in the band sticking out jauntily. Two long, blonde braids come down over my breasts. I am smiling, leaning slightly on one leg, my hands clasped in front of me. There is an innocence in my round, soft face. A look that says I am happy to be here, this is my place.

Years ago a college friend came to Salt Lake City to ski and to stay with us. My mother had placed the picture on a bookshelf in the living room. He looked at it, took it up in both hands to get a better view, and turning to me with a curious look in his face, as if he had only then realized something terribly important–he said, "It's you. This is you. It's perfect." For him, the picture stilled me, *distilled* me, represented me as I *really* am, as he saw me, as he wanted me to be. Fishergirl. It is a picture that I want to show friends, and a picture that I want to hide. When I look at it now, I feel like an impostor. Fishergirl. It is me, and it isn't me. It was me, and it wasn't me. It always has been me and never will be me.

It was my father who taught me how to fly fish. And it was I who eagerly learned, never imagining that later, as a grown woman, the teaching would begin to feel like a molding. Never imagining that Fishergirl would grow to eclipse me, throwing a shadow over the many selves I wanted to become. I want to know, how much of me is this fishing girl and how much of that fishing girl is only borrowed, made up and put on? How much of Fishergirl is a sacrifice to my father's dream of a daughter, to my friends' desires for an eccentric companion, and how much is my own choice, my own desire? I want to let go of Fishergirl, shed her like a delicate snaky skin and start all over, making her up again, all by myself, as I go along.

On the train I lie with my head on a small, white pillow against the window, my curled body rocking, rocking with the rhythm of the moving cars. Even nested like this, I am restless. As always, I am disturbed by going home to the West, if not on the surface, then in the depths. It is only partly the severe landscape, the rocky dry March. I am agitated in the flesh-and-bone home of my body. The lost feeling started way back when the train left Chicago and is worse now. I get up and move through the train cars, descending to the lower level, furtively opening a window wide enough to feel fresh air on my face.

In transit, between one life and another, I forget who I am. I suffer again from an inexplicable loathing. "Let me out of this body," a voice inside me growls. My soul wants to take flight before we reach my destination. For a moment it is all I can do to stop from tearing myself limb from limb. In the train restroom, I wash my hands and face, lingering over my cheekbones as I dry them. "You," I say to myself in the mirror, "You are a pretty girl. Remember who you are." I look at my breasts, rounded under a rumpled blue T-shirt, my nipples showing through the thin cotton. I feel them being touched, gently by a woman I love. I remember that I am loved. I remember that this is one of the beautiful and distinctive things about a woman, her breasts. Slowly, I come back into myself.

When I return to my seat I pull from my red backpack a book my friend Cate gave me, *The River Why* by David James Duncan. It is a book about fishing for people who don't fish. Such books abound. For Father's Day one year I sent my father a copy of Norman Maclean's *A River Runs Through It*. My father and I exchanged letters about the book. He liked it but was tired of books that pretended to be about fishing and were really about politics or love instead. Once he visited me in St. Paul and on my shelf found a copy of Richard Brautigan's *Trout Fishing in America*, a bawdy, political book about love and sex and fly fishing; a commentary on the quality of life in America and how we treat nature. He looked through a couple of pages and said to me, almost angrily, "This isn't about fishing. This is crap."

I told him, "See, Trout Fishing in America is a guy, a man. It's a spoof on the myth and ideal of trout fishing." When Brautigan goes trout fishing he feels like a telephone repairman. He catches grotesque fish, not beautiful gleaming ones, but fish with ugly tumors and eyes half hanging out.

"It's supposed to be funny and ironic," I said again.

"I haven't seen anything funny yet," he said, shutting the book and putting Brautigan back on the shelf.

I open *The River Why* and start to read. Cate had given it to me nearly a year earlier, soon after we met. Inside the front cover she wrote in the lovely and difficult-to-decipher script that still amuses me, "Gretchen–about fishing and love and other matters of the heart–with great affection this Easter Day, 1993." We had known each other only a month. We had never been fishing together. We had only watched movies and talked, eaten at restaurants, browsed antique stores. She had never seen me with a fishing pole in my hand. She had never seen me in a pair of waders. On our first date I dressed in a black leather miniskirt and jacket. Underneath I wore black fishnet pantyhose and a white, nearly transparent tank top. My hair was freshly cut, clean on the back and sides and long enough on top to stand straight up. I waited for her on the sidewalk outside the restaurant, leaning with studied casualness against the brick of the building, my eyes shaded by sunglasses. When she arrived she daringly kissed me on the mouth in front of passing cars and couples strolling by.

After our date she gave me a note with a chocolate trout attached. The note said, "For Gretchen T. Legler, Fishergirl." The chocolate trout was covered in gaudy, bright foil. The note went on: "You are such a work. So rugged and graceful and raw and polished and pure. You are like a river through me. Everything seems fluid and everything possible." Already to her, even then, despite my leather miniskirt, despite the shades, despite my urban *machisma*, I was Fishergirl. She, too, was imagining me this way from the very beginning. How is it, I want to know, that we become who we are in other people's minds, and exactly how true are their visions of us? Who invented Fishergirl, and why does she stay with me?

Cate loved one specific part of the book and had marked it for me–a poem by William Butler Yeats, "The Song of Wandering Aengus." The poem for me is about many things, but mostly about desire–the pursuit of a vision of oneself, the pursuit of the *possibility* of self, of joy. It goes like this:

> *I went out to the hazel wood,*
> *Because a fire was in my head,*
> *And cut and peeled a hazel wand,*
> *And hooked a berry on a thread;*
> *And when white moths were on the wing,*
> *And moth-like stars were flickering out,*
> *I dropped the berry in the stream*
> *And caught a little silver trout.*
>
> *When I had laid it on the floor*
> *I went to blow the fire aflame,*
> *But something rustled on the floor,*
> *And some one called me by my name:*
> *It had become a glimmering girl*
> *With apple blossoms in her hair*
> *Who called me by my name and ran*
> *And faded through the brightening air.*
>
> *Though I am old with wandering*
> *Through hollow lands and hilly lands,*
> *I will find out where she has gone,*
> *And kiss her lips, and take her hands,*
> *And walk along long dappled grass,*
> *And pluck till time and times are done,*
> *The silver apples of the moon,*
> *The golden apples of the sun.*

The River Why is about a fishing family made up of Mister Fly Fisherman himself, Henning Hale-Orviston; Ma, an inveterate bait angler, and their sons Gus and Bill Bob, both of whom suffer minor emotional problems and act out rebelliously as a result of their parents' constant dueling over the relative merits of bait and flies. Henning, you see, wants his son Gus to be a fly fisherman. Ma, on the other hand, wants her son to catch as many fish as possible on the crudest of baits. She is happiest when he catches a record bass on a rotten wiener. The book is not really about fishing at all, but a setting for a story about love and spirituality and finding your own way in life–finding a way that is your own, finding a path that is not any path anyone has expected for you, laid for you or mapped for you. It is about finding out who you are. Who you are. Who you are. Who you are.

The train is making its way through a canyon along the Green River in Colorado. Hit now with late afternoon sun, the steep rocky walls are golden. As I try to read, I also listen to a family in the seats across from me. There is a little boy and a little girl. The parents are young and attractive. They laugh, they look each other in the eye, wink at each other and consult often about what they should do or will do or just did with the kids. "Case and I are going to the potty," the father says, as they head off down the stairs hand in hand. The little girl is standing up on the seat looking out the window. The mother says, "It's pretty out there, isn't it, with the sun on the rocks?" The little girl says, "Yes, and the river is pretty, too." I look out and see a fly fisherman, knee-deep in the river, and a naked man, lolling in a tiny tub made with rocks to hold a steaming hot spring. Both the fly fisher and the bather are waving at us.

My mother is at the train station waiting for me, nervously scanning the train windows, watching the passengers getting off. But I make it across the platform and have her in my arms before she sees me. I am struck again by how small she feels, even wrapped in a sweater and parka against the late spring night. I am small, too, but feel beefy and huge compared to her.

It is well after midnight as we drive up from the valley and toward the mountains, toward Mt. Olympus, at the base of which my parents' house nearly lies. In my mother's kitchen, around the table, the room lit by the white light of the stove top, we talk. We lean close to one another and whisper so as not to disturb my father, who was not up to greet me, but is sleeping in the basement in my brothers' old room. My mother reminds me not to flush the toilet upstairs because it will wake my father.

She tells me she has started doing something called container gardening. She points to two pots on the table, full of tiny plants. She is always starting something new, always following a new lead. She doesn't let herself get in a rut, become defined by the things that she does. Once I finally got used to the idea of saying, "My mother is a potter," she stopped making pots. Now she does container gardening, watches birds and grows herbs and roses. She has finally grown a perfect rose, she tells me. So perfect, so deep red, so velvety was this Lincoln Rose, that she brought it to work to show it off. "It may never happen again," she says. "I had to show it to someone."

The day before we leave for our trip, my mother and I shop and pack. Not only are we shopping for ourselves, but my mother is trying to get the house in order for my father as well. She has gone to three grocery stores, all far away from one another, to purchase his favorite muffins, biodegradable toilet paper and canned spaghetti with meat. She buys carrots and celery and cuts all the vegetables into thin strips and puts them in small Ziploc bags for his lunches. Then she makes lasagna for our dinner. During a normal week she will do all of this and spend eight hours a day working as a secretary. My mother's life makes me tired. She is sixty-three years old.

My father wants to spend time with me on this morning before we leave. First, he talks to me about his computer, his "Power-Book," how it is the best computer he's ever bought and I should consider buying one, too. He then takes me on a tour of his new inventions. "Here," he says, "is my snow melter for the cabin." It is a big garbage can with a brass faucet pushed into the side. He opens the back of his truck to show me his new winch. He shows me his bicycles. I feel as if I am watching a kid open toys at Christmas. He asks me if I would like to ride to the store with him to get some glue. I say, "No, Mom and I have things to pack yet," and he turns away from me gloomily.

Between packing and shopping, I wander around my parents' house, as I always do when I am home, looking to see what is new and what is still the same as it always was. I open the door to my father's office. Once it really was an office, piled with paper and books, but long ago it was turned into a fly-tying and rod-building room. Now the room has an eerie abandoned feel, as if he got up one day and walked away from it, leaving all these artifacts behind. When my parents bought their land in Montana, my father stopped fishing so much. He stopped tying flies and became obsessed, instead, with building a cabin. His interests now are focused on composting toilets, solar power, battery banks and wells. He is the first president of the Landowners' Association and spends much of his time mediating disputes between city slickers who, like him, bought thirty-acre parcels of the subdivided ranch their property is part of.

My mother warned me about the office. "I don't like to go in there," she said. "I think there may be black-widow spiders in the corners." When I open the door a rich and thick smell meets my nose—a smell of the skins of birds and old, old smoke. The walls are still thickly covered with plastic bags of fly-tying material hanging from hooks; peacock herl, rabbit fur, skins of mallards and wood ducks, tinsel and bright yarn, packages of turkey quills, pheasant necks, swatches of deer hair. The shelves are lined with tidy chests containing pullout boxes of hooks, bottles of glue, tweezers and other small tools. Several fly-tying vises still are clamped to the edge of the desk. And from every surface sprout flies–elaborate streamers, tiny imitation mosquitoes, deer-hair grass-hoppers of varying sizes, scrubby-looking nymphs and elegant Royal Coachmans.

He had tried to teach me to tie flies. He gave me a book on fly tying for Christmas one year: *Jack Dennis' Western Trout Fly-Tying Manual.* Inside the cover it was inscribed "To Gretty from Daddy, Christmas 1986. I hope you will find this as useful as I did. You must still learn the basics first." I was twenty-six then. I never learned even the basics. The flies I did tie have all unraveled in my fly box.

That night around the dinner table it's mostly my father talking and me listening. My mother is quietly eating, sipping icy tonic water from a tall glass. She gets up and serves my father more lasagna when he asks for it. He talks about being close to retiring from his job as a professor and how university people are hovering, like vultures, waiting to move in on his space. He feels angry. He has worked hard and wants to be respected. It isn't fair, and I tell him so. In these rare moments when despite everything I see his fear, my heart opens to him. But it never stays open long enough to make anything change.

Still later, after we have spent some time talking about how I will be moving to Alaska soon, my father clears his throat and says, "I'd like to come up there and fish with you." A tiny, cramped part of my heart smirks. Fat chance, I think. I am moving to a new place, with a chance to start all over, a new life, and already he wants to come and fish with me. Already I am going there to be Fishergirl. What about the rest of it, I want to ask him. I am also going to Alaska to work, to start my first job as a professor of English and creative writing. I will be a teacher, like him. A writer. A member of a new community. I will be meeting people, dating, buying a home, maybe even building a log cabin. I will be so much more and other than Fishergirl. I want to smother my own desire to be Fishergirl and even suffer the damage I do to myself in the process, all to finally wreck this rickety bridge that joins us, to wipe away this part of me that feels so made by him.

We started out fishing as a family, my two brothers, my sister and I, my mother and my father. At first we fished from a small aluminum boat at big artificial lakes around Salt Lake–Strawberry Reservoir, Deer Creek. We fished for trout and perch, trolling big red and white lures. Or we fished from shore with worms and corn. We made jigs in the basement, pouring hot lead into tiny molds, then dressing up the jigs with black and yellow feathers. In the beginning we had trout in the freezer. We had trout for breakfast. We had trout in the sink, still wet and gleaming, just taken off the stringer. For years we fished this way.

Then things began to change, and we didn't have so much fish around anymore. Fishing became more about art than food. Both of my parents became interested in fly fishing. It was my mother who started tying flies, ordering great quantities of feathers and thread and vises and scissors and glue from *Herter's* magazine. At first we still used spinning reels, attaching the flies to lines rigged with water-filled clear bubbles so that we could cast them out far into the mountain lakes we backpacked to.

Fishing in our family gradually became more and more specialized, until tying flies and building rods became my father's hobby. My father took a special interest in teaching me to fly fish. For me, as a teenager, it was something romantic and different. I made a transition, a leap into a new identity, that summer at Yellowstone, the summer my brother took the picture of me–I changed from a silly, ordinary girl with no boyfriends and straight A's on my report card into Fishergirl. The fishing will never be as good for me as it was that summer. My father would walk with me to the stream edge, pointing to pools where he said he knew there were fish. He showed me how to cast, keeping my fly line up in the air, throwing out enough line to get my fly to the shaded, cool bank on the opposite side. Then he would leave me to fish alone.

I caught cutthroat after cutthroat, moving slowly down the stream, fishing the big pools and the noisy shallow riffles, too. Sun warmed the back of my neck, the air was dense with the sound of snapping grasshoppers and the smell of sage and pine, all mixed with the coolness rising up from the stream. Nothing then could have done me any harm. When I'd caught so many fish that my imitation grasshopper was frayed, I changed to something colorful and big. I didn't know the names, and I wasn't picky. I'd cast the fly upstream and watch its big wings float quickly down, my body tensed for the sight of a swirl, the popping sound of a trout's lips pulling my fly down into the water. Once, a voice startled me, "You're a natural, you know," and I turned around to find my father sitting on the gravel, his back against the cutbank, smoking a cigarette and watching me. "Do you like this?" he asked me then. I told him there was no place else in the world I would rather be.

The morning my mother and I finally leave for our road trip, my father is sitting in the kitchen with his portable computer and Post-it notes and pens of different colors. He props the computer up next to his cereal bowl and works. My mother reminds me he needs to be where it is light and cheery. He needs the sun, she says, or he gets depressed. But it means there is no room for her. She finally told him, she says, not to put his stuff out on weekend mornings when she is home. He does it anyway, and when she comes in he says, "Do you want me to move now?"

We tell him we're going to leave at seven in the morning. "Maybe you will, maybe you won't," he says crossly. I am finishing my last cup of coffee before we get in the car. My father and I are standing at the kitchen window, looking out at their cat, Bilbo, who is sitting awkwardly, one arthritic leg sticking out at a right angle, in a shaft of dusty sunshine on the balcony.

He asks me if I know how old Bilbo is. I say no, I can't remember when we got her. He looks me in the eye and says soberly, "Bilbo is twenty years old." I am appropriately amazed.

"She doesn't do much anymore," he says. "She likes to sit in the sun and sleep mostly. She's slowing down." He seems saddened by this, but also comforted, as if the cat is doing just exactly what an old cat, or an old person, should be doing–slowing down, enjoying what he or she loves best. The conversation makes me wonder about my father, about my mother, about how much time I have left with my parents. I guess twenty years, maybe. That's only a handful. I can imagine these years with my mother, but no clear picture of the woman I am now comes to me with my father in it.

I became my father's fishing pal. Some mornings I would be awakened so early that I cried as I tied my bootlaces, not wanting to go on yet another fishing trip, not wanting to go out into the cold morning. But later, on the water, as we motored through thick fog, and when I brought home a twenty-inch rainbow trout with a story about how it grabbed my red and white Dare-Devil when the lure had just hit the water, I felt sure that this was who I was. Fishergirl. When I was older we would go on Sunday trips, sometimes with my brother Austin, but many times alone. We would drive up out of Salt Lake, past Park City, into the mountains to fish shallow, rocky streams.

Somehow we became locked into a vision of one another as Fishergirl and her dad. I knew hardly anything else about him except this. For Father's Day I would send him wood duck skins, or trout napkins, or mugs with fish for handles. For Christmas he gave me boxes of leader material, little leather envelopes with sheep fleece linings for storing flies, small scissors attached to retractable cords for clipping fly line while standing up to your waist in water. One Christmas I opened package after package of fly-fishing gadgets. There was a zippered leather envelope full of half a dozen dazzling streamers, a brooch made out of a huge and elaborate fly, a mobile of a trout and flies, a little pad of fly line cleaner, a spool of fly line. Mary, my brother's girlfriend, handed me another package, this one wrapped in lavender and tied with a turquoise bow. She winked at me. "This is for you, Gretty, because you're a woman, too." Inside the box was a bar of scented soap, body powder and bath oil. Mary winked at me again, as if to say, he sometimes forgets.

When my mother and I leave exactly at seven, my father is in the shower where he can't possibly say goodbye. He went in there as we were heading out the door. I want him to be different. I want him to help us carry out our bags, to help load them into the car, to hug us each goodbye and kiss us on the cheek, to wish us good luck and good fun and to stand in the driveway and wave as we drive off into the morning. This may never happen. I can't depend on his changing.

Five hours later, my mother and I arrive at Hovenweep, our first stop. We walk down into a shaded valley, perfumed with sand dust and sage. The bluffs above the valley are ringed with dilapidated sandstone houses, put together brick by brick centuries ago. My mother needs to stop often. Her doctors won't treat her cough, she says, with some amount of anger. They just tell her to quit smoking. This walking is hard on her, but we go at her pace and I am in no hurry. We spend our first night at a hotel owned by a German woman and her husband in Cortez, Colorado. We get a message at the desk that someone has called for us. It was my father. We left an explicit itinerary with phone numbers so he knows exactly where we are. My mother calls home, and my father wants to know where the catfood is for Bilbo.

On the second day we go to the Four Corners and take goofy pictures. In one I am doing a Twister pose with my hands and feet in all four states and my mother's shadow is cast across me. At the Four Corners we both buy jewelry. My mother is gracious and kind to the Navajo women artists. She made pots for so long, and for so long sold them for not even half of the work she put into them. She knows how hard this kind of work is. "I love your work," she tells the women, and she smiles.

Before we go to Mesa Verde we visit the Anasazi Heritage Center. As we walk around the center, my mother coughs. I go from exhibit to exhibit looking at baskets under glass, a whole pithouse reassembled, panoramas, diagrams, collections of arrowheads and artists' reconstructions of pueblo life. As I walk I hear her cough echo through the museum.

At Mesa Verde, we walk down to Spruce House. We are guided by a ranger who doesn't lie to us. He reminds me of Burl Ives–he has red hair and a red beard, a big belly and a deep, friendly voice. His story about the ancient people is full of holes. "We really don't know exactly why they built in this canyon," he says. "Some people say for protection against marauding enemies. But you know, that's a particular idea that may be more about us than about them. These are only educated guesses." He asks us to speculate about the tiny houses built up in the thin wedges of the cliff. "Privacy," someone says. "Lookouts," someone else says. He smiles and suggests that in such close quarters maybe lovers used these huts as places to be together. This idea appeals to me.

At the visitors' center I buy a book called *Our Trip to Mesa Verde, 1922*, a chronicle of four girls' trip to Mesa Verde in 1922. The girls, who were friends and schoolteachers, hiked the whole way from Ouray, Colorado, to Mesa Verde and back, to see the cliff houses that were just then being excavated and opened to the public. Ruth E., Ruth H., Dot and Fetzie were their names. How unordinary they must have been, four girls alone, hiking through the sage, in 1922. I envy them their bravery. I want to be like that. In the pictures they look wonderful and flamboyant in tall lace-up boots and dusty trousers, floppy hats and old-fashioned packs. The trip took them a month. In the epilogue, written in

1988, Ruth E. writes that each one of them married and they all lived happily ever after.

At the hotel in Durango, Colorado, we joke with the two young women who are behind the desk. They are tanned and clear-faced with perfect teeth and wide mouths. Their eyes are bright. My mother asks if there have been any phone calls for us. I joke that we're on the run. "Thelma and Louise," my mother says, smiling at them and winking. The girls laugh. For dinner we eat at an Italian restaurant. For dessert my mother has custard with raspberry cordial sauce and wants the recipe from the waiter. She vows when we get home she will buy a cookbook to reproduce this dessert.

While we are getting ready for bed, my mother tells me that her arthritis is so bad now she can hardly pull on her pantyhose anymore. But, she says wryly, "The good thing about getting old is learning to accept yourself." I keep seeing her in a picture from long ago when she used to be a model. In the picture she wears a black short skirt, waist jacket and pillbox hat. For a time, when we were young, my mother tried to teach Ally and me how to be ladies. She bought us each a pair of white gloves. She taught us how to roll on pantyhose. "Always wear your gloves when you put on your hose," she said, "or you'll put runs in them." Ally and I walked around the living room with books balanced on our heads, practicing good posture. She wanted me to learn to walk with my feet straight, not sticking out to the sides like a duck. She showed us how to turn, like models on a fashion runway.

Most weekends, when I was young, we went fishing. We would drive through mountain valleys, and at every bridge or roadside rest, my father would get out and look at the water. Mostly we were all bored silly, fidgeting in the back seat of the car. But there was also a part of me that paid attention when he would stop the car on the side of the road, walk over to the streamside or look down on it from the bridge, and come back with a report. "Seems high," he'd say. At the next one he'd stop the car, get out, come back, "Seems muddy," he'd say. And again, "Looks clear."

This is one of the reasons I signed on as Fishergirl in the first place. I wanted to be like this–to be interested in and knowledgeable about one thing. His love of streams, of fishing, seemed so complete and pure and mysterious. He knew something we didn't, and I wanted to know what it was. I wanted to learn how to find fish, how to tell a good stream from a bad one, how not to frighten a trout in the water, what fly to use. Mostly I wanted to know what it was that he loved so much. I wanted to experience that, too, to love something so utterly you assumed everyone else was as fascinated with it as you.

I took my fly rods with me to college. I had two, both safely traveling in black plastic tubes, with my name on them in gold tape. Gretchen T. Legler. My father had made both of the rods for me and the carrying tubes. I stored the rods in my dorm room, in the back of the closet. No one I knew at college wanted to fish. But they all liked the idea that I had fly rods in the back of my closet. It made me interesting. A professor of mine flattered me by giving me a fly tying kit–a big metal box filled with clear plastic drawers. In each drawer was something new–hooks of different sizes, colored thread and tinsel, feathers, hair, yarn and glue. He had bought it thinking he'd get into fly fishing, he said. But he had never opened it. I have moved the kit around with me to six different homes and apartments. I've never used it either.

One weekend in college I could not bear the city a moment longer and headed off to the rolling green hills of southern Minnesota to fish. I did some research and got the trout stream maps from the Minnesota Department of Natural Resources. I thought I knew exactly where I was going. As I drove along the dirt roads in the hot and heavy humid air, I slowly passed a black Amish buggy. Two little boys in flat straw hats grinned and waved at me. Their father, driving, nodded as I passed them. I was proud and feeling independent, feeling like Fishergirl.

I drove around all day looking for the stream that looked just right—something wide and deep, like the streams in Utah and Wyoming. But these streams confused me. They were all thin and muddy and covered over by trees. How would you fish a stream like this? A kind of indecision had seized me. I realized that this was no fun at all. The whole activity lost its meaning. I drove back to the city, to my dorm room and my books. I had not even wetted my line. I felt somehow stupid and false, as if I wasn't cut out for this at all, as if without my father by my side, I was no Fishergirl at all. I wanted to be solid unto myself and, instead, I felt full of holes.

When my mother and I leave Durango, we head off in the wrong direction. All the while we are driving happily and talking. We talk about her pottery. She tries to explain to me that the pots themselves were never her goal. That the whole thing was about process. And when she stopped making pots, it wasn't as if she had stopped being herself. She just moved on to something new.

Pottery defined her for me for so long. She was always in the garage working with a mound of clay on her wheel, loading her kiln, or in the kitchen with a pot on the table, rubbing the outside with a wooden spoon to make it shine. Her pots were mostly hand-built. She was trying, she said, to replicate Anasazi methods and designs. There was always clay on the doorknobs, clay on the phone.

Now she's stopped. She tells me that my father keeps asking her when she'll get back to pottery. "Maybe never," she tells him. She says to him, "I'm just not interested anymore." Now the garage is full of his tools and gadgets, and the kiln is on the back porch under a tarp. "What do you mean you're not interested anymore?" he asks her. She tells him that she is changing, that's it, and that he has changed, too; after all, he quit tying flies.

My mother and I get to Silverton before I realize we are going the wrong way. I tell her sheepishly that we need to turn around.

She heads back up over the pass on the curving road we've just come down. It is cold on top of the pass. There is a lot of snow. It is beautiful. She tells me that she dreams about being on an endless road and coming to crevasse after crevasse and turning around. "This has something to do with life," she says, her eyes on the road, both hands on the wheel.

We talk about my being a lesbian. She tells me that since I told her this about myself she has discovered that everywhere she turns there is a lesbian or a gay man–an author, a friend, a movie star and ordinary people, too. The letter I wrote to my parents, in which I revealed the reason I had left my husband, was boring and full of platitudes. It was full of short, declarative sentences. I had been careful with every word, every phrase. I wanted them both to understand plainly, with no flourishes, what had happened to me, how I had changed, how I had emerged. The letter had nothing in it of the joy I felt at the time. I was unaccustomed to the language of joy. The very word "joy" felt awkward in my hands. I had hardly a vocabulary to express myself, whereas I had practiced for years the language of grief. "I am so happy," I told my parents in the letter. That is the word I repeated over and over and over. Happy. Happy. Happy. Only my mother understood. She turns to me now in the car and says, "You seem happier."

My mother telephoned as soon as she got my letter. I was sitting at the kitchen table by an open window. There was sun shining in. Cate sat next to me in a chair, holding my hand with both of hers. My mother did not say much. I had to chip loose what I wanted from her. I asked, "Are you surprised?"

"Yes and no."

"Are you sad?"

"Yes."

"Why?"

"The world is so unpredictable. Things hardly ever go anymore as you expect."

I was quiet.

"I have been thinking about how much it takes to raise a child," she said. "And I think we always did the right thing, but maybe not." She paused and then said, "I know we always did stop for ice cream."

Afterward, exhausted, I lay down in bed next to Cate and we slept. It had been easier than I had imagined, telling my mother. She had said all of the right things. "We still love you," she had said. But still, I was overcome by a deep weariness all mixed up with sadness and a clear sense of being suddenly released from a great, sagging weight. I was free. Free. Free of something. What? Free to do what? Be what? In my sleep I dreamed of my sister, Ally. I dreamed I was holding her hand, and I woke with Cate's hand in mine. I slept again, and awoke again when I heard someone call me by my name. Still, Cate was sound asleep beside me. "Gretchen," the voice said, only once and very clear.

As my mother drives, I ask her why my father never called me about the letter. "I'll tell you, but you won't like it," she says. "He said he didn't care as long as you didn't tell everybody. He thinks sexual proclivities are private things."

"Oh," I say.

"And he never read your letter."

My heart lands like a stone in my chest.

"He worries about you," she tells me, "that it will be hard for you to be happy like this. That it will be hard for you to get a job." I laugh. My life has never been this easy. I have finally claimed space for myself against the forces that work to keep us all from knowing who we are; the forces that keep us pasting ourselves together from the fragments of other people's desires. Of course, I think, he would never read my letter. He wouldn't understand it, and it would frighten him.

There is another picture of me fly fishing. This time in color, taken by Craig when we were still married. In it I am wearing a bright-red flannel shirt. On my head is the same old hat, adorned with a different feather–still long and gray, something I picked up along a stream or in the woods, vowing that I'd place it in my hat and never forget where it came from. My fly rod is tucked under one arm, and in my other hand I am holding a shining, flickering cutthroat trout upside down by the tail. I learned all this from my father. When you get the fish, you pull in line enough so you have the fish under control; then you pull your bandanna from your vest, wet it, and taking the fish gently by its strong tail, lift it out of the water and carefully take the fly out of its mouth. Before you had even started to fish, you had clipped the barb off of the hook so that the fish's mouth would be hurt as little as possible. Then you let the fish go, first holding it by its tail in the stream until it has got its wits back and can swim away.

On the day this picture was taken, Craig caught an extraordinary fish. We had seen it lurking in the shade under the opposite bank, and Craig worked all morning to get it to strike. He played the fish too long, however, and by the time it was unhooked the fish was frail. And when he released it, the fish turned over on its back, its white belly open to the sky. Craig was cradling it in his palms in the water when my father appeared around the bend. He showed Craig how to resuscitate a fish by moving it slowly back and forth in the water, forcing oxygen into its gills. He did this with his big, intelligent hands until the fish flipped its tail and swam strongly upstream. Craig told me, jokingly, that he was lucky. He only caught fish when my father was there to see it. He seemed to understand so quickly something I had felt painfully all my life, that being good at fishing somehow wins my father's respect.

On one of our first dates, I took Craig to Hay Creek, a tiny trout stream in southern Minnesota. I wanted to impress Craig, so in preparation for the trip I called my father for advice. I told him that I didn't know how to fish these little Minnesota streams, and he told me I should use wet flies. Nymphs. He sent me a gift of a small packet of fluorescent green and orange "strike indicators," bits of colored foam tape you tear off and stick on your leader when you are using a nymph. You watch the strike indicator and when it stops moving, odds are your nymph is being nibbled by a trout. I hear his voice, "My nymph fishing improved about fifty percent when I started using strike indicators."

On that trip, Craig and I fished in ankle-deep water, catching two small trout; then we spread out a blanket beside the stream for our lunch. We played, putting grapes in each other's mouths, feeding each other sliced apples and cheese, and then started to kiss, finally making slow love in the tall grass. I saw sky over his back. I heard birds and the water. I smelled warm dust from the road. We washed naked in the cold stream, and I teased him that this was a risky idea he had had, what with the road so near. "It was your idea, too," he said, smiling.

Craig took a picture of me on that trip that he later had a friend of ours make into a watercolor painting. I often think that it is only partly an image of me that emerged on that photographic paper; the rest is Craig's vision of me, fed by his love. The painting hung above our bed, until after we divorced and Craig gave it back to me–my shining face and blue, blue eyes, a green shirt, a green hat and a yellow daisy in the hatband. In the painting, I look like a wood sprite. I look like Fishergirl.

My mother and I are winding our way toward Chaco Canyon on the third day of our trip. We take a thin, rutted dirt road, so narrow in places and hemmed in by red rock that I wonder if the car will fit through. It is early in the season and the road hasn't been graded yet. All the ruins here are in the canyon bottom, not up in the cliffs. Pueblo Bonito, the largest ruin in the canyon, is said to have been a mecca, a cultural and political center, crawling with people, surrounded by farms. There are roads carved in the sandstone, going up over the red rock sides of the canyon and leading to other pueblos. One story is that Pueblo Bonito got too large. There were a couple of bad years. Everyone died or moved. I want to know where the people went. I want to know what happened to their lives, their individual, private lives.

I tell my mother I am finally beginning to figure out my life. I am realizing that there are doors that will not always be open to me. I feel as if I am becoming wise, that my youth is ending. She looks at me and says quietly, "People talk about finding the meaning of life. People used to know what the meaning of life was–a job and a place to live and enough to eat. Life has gotten so complicated."

We talk about my father. She tells me that before my visit, my father asked especially for her to sit and talk to him about something important. They sat, one on each end of the kitchen table, and he told her that he was worried about my visit. He was worried that I would be difficult. Difficult. I would ask hard questions. I would rebel in small, insignificant ways. I would frustrate him by sleeping in late in the mornings, waking only after he had left the house, by staying up late, talking with my mother in the kitchen long after he had gone to bed, and by crying. "He always makes you cry," my mother has said on other visits. "I hope he doesn't make you cry. You don't have to let him make you cry."

My mother tells me that my father wants to spend time with me. "He wants to spend time with you *alone*," she says. "He tells me that he hasn't spent time with you alone in three years." Alone for what, I want to ask. Even when we are alone together, the space between us is like a vast canyon that our voices barely carry across. The last time we were alone together, we went fishing at my parents' cabin in Montana. We packed lunches and water and hiked down the steep slope to the Madison River. As we put on our wading gear and tied on flies, he talked to me about my mother. He said he loved her and didn't want her to die before he did.

"Have you told her that?" I asked.

"Not in so many words," he said. "There's no doubt in my mind. Unless I get hit by a car, I will outlive your mother."

He left me at the first pool. I watched him tromping downstream in his waders and fishing vest, his rod tip bobbing as he stepped over grassy hummocks, until he disappeared around the first big bend. I tied on a fly, something big with white wings that I could see easily in the fast water, and listlessly cast out and drew in line for two hours. My father, I knew, would be catching fish. He would be taking up netfuls of river water, scientifically determining the insects the fish were eating, and then finding (or tying) an exact match.

When he came back to join me at lunchtime, he found me lying in the sun, reading a mystery novel. Beside me I had a stack of reeds I had collected for my mother, who wanted them to thatch the roofs of the birdhouses my father had been building from hollowed-out logs. He set his rod down in the grass and took a sip of water. He asked me, "Have you ever thought we were rich?" I said no. "Well, we're not rich. We never have been. But Mother has done an incredible job managing our finances, so we have a good ratio of income to outflow and a good retirement." I asked if he had told her that. "Not in so many words," he said. "I'm tempted to ask her to show me how to do it. I'm going to need to know." I want to ask him with what words or what actions he *has* told her that he loves her. I want to ask him if he loves me.

On the fourth day my mother and I leave Gallup and go to Window Rock on the Navajo Reservation. We stop at the Hubbell Trading Post and visit a shop where Navajo women are weaving. My mother wants to talk to them, but they only smile at her. She looks at a young woman standing nearby and says to her, "I guess I don't speak their language. Can you ask them how long it takes them to weave one of these rugs?" The young woman says something to the older women, and then turns to my mother and says, "These women are in their seventies. They only speak *Dine*. They never went to school. They were old-fashioned and stayed home all of their lives, you know. It takes them hundreds of hours to weave a blanket." When we leave, my mother thanks the old weavers and the young woman who was her interpreter. My mother is one of the nicest people I know.

*   *   *

In the beginning I liked that fly fishing with my father made me feel somehow superior to people who fished with spinning gear and bait. I felt as if I had evolved into a more refined and more intelligent creature when I learned to fly fish. I would laugh at the jokes my father would make about hayseeds who fished with corn and cheese balls. But after a while the jokes didn't seem funny anymore. On one particular trip I remember feeling ashamed and putting the shame in my pocket like a shell or a tiny pinecone.

My father and brother and I had set out on an already hot, dry morning for the lower part of Slough Creek in Yellowstone. We had taken a short cut over a steep hill, into the woods, where we often saw moose and deer. Far away, up higher on the green meadows, we had heard elk bugle. Along the way we met a horse-drawn wagon taking this route to a dude ranch north of the park. We got to the stream, and there was no one there yet. As we sat on a log by the very first pool, quiet at that time of day, still and amber-colored, we peeled off our boots and wool socks and put on waders and wading shoes and got our fly rods set. I was missing something, as always, and had to ask for it—some tippet, some leader, maybe a few extra flies. My father handed them over impatiently, as if to say, you're old enough now to have your fishing vest in order.

As we were preparing to fish, a father and son arrived, talking loudly, breaking the still. And my father muttered under his voice as they moved away, walking merrily along the high grassy bank, that they would scare the fish, that they shouldn't be allowed here with their spinning gear and flashing, hook-heavy lures. I told him in the kind of controlled, angry voice in which I was learning to speak with him, "It isn't our stream." He looked at me and smiled and said, "Yes, it is." Instead of feeling fine and laughing, I just felt snobbish, and I knew it wasn't right.

We are headed to Canyon de Chelly. My mother describes a movie to me about a woman and a man who fall in love. He's an ex-con. The man and woman kiss in the movie. It is their first kiss, tentative and full of passion. She could feel the passion, she says, the electricity. She hasn't felt that way in a long time.

"Is that what you feel?" she asks me, tentatively.

"You mean with a woman?"

"Yes," she says.

"Yes," I answer. "Now more than ever before." I try to explain this to her. "It wasn't that I never had great sex with men," I say. "It's that with them, with men, I was never fully present in my own body." She tells me that she is surprised and a little embarrassed that I talk so easily about sex.

At Canyon de Chelly we walk down into the wash to see the White House Ruins. I keep handing my mother my water bottle and urging her to drink. "Water is good for you," I say. It is a steep walk, and she goes slowly. At the bottom there is thin spring grass and a hogan, and red walls rising up to blue cloudless sky. We walk along the wash in the deep sand to the ruins, where there are other people who have come down in four-wheel-drive vehicles with Navajo guides.

At the ruins some women have spread out blankets and are selling jewelry. I buy a silver medallion, shaped like the sun, on a leather string. Coming up from the bottom of the canyon, my mother takes a picture of me in my blue jeans and ribbed, sleeveless undershirt, the medallion around my neck. In the picture I imagine coming from this shot, I look hot and tanned. I am smiling. My breasts show rounded under my shirt. This will be a sexy picture. Cate will like this, I think. I have never felt this way about my body before–recognizing it as desirable. It is the same body I have always had, but I am different in it now.

The last stop my mother and I make is in Kayenta, Arizona. As we drive there, night is coming on and the clouds above us turn slowly from pink to peach to gold. The clouds are so close and the color so intense that I feel as if we are rising up into them, as if we are flying, as if at any moment we will burst through this blanket of gold and be soaring among stars in a blue-black sky. At the hotel we have Navajo fry bread and salad for dinner. Just to watch her order from a menu, to see her make a choice about what it is that she wants, such a simple choice, gives me a feeling of great intimacy. Neither one of us sleeps well. Clearly, we don't want to go home.

As we drive through Monument Valley the next morning, the sun comes up deep burnt-orange behind the weird sandstone sculptures of the valley. My mother keeps saying to me that this is the best vacation she has ever had. "You're easy to be with," she says. She is surprised by the things I do for her, such as open doors and carry her suitcase. "You are so polite," she says.

When we get back to Salt Lake she wants to have our pictures developed right away. We drop them off at the camera counter at Safeway, even before we reach home, and rush back to get them exactly an hour later. We show them to my father. He looks at three or four and puts the stack aside.

There is another picture of me fly fishing. I am older still. Maybe thirty. I stand in a wide, curving stream with my fly rod, casting out into the silver water with trees rising behind me and gray-blue mountains beyond that. The picture looks romantic and perfect: girl and stream. Mountains. Fish. But I remember this time. I remember my heavy pack, the black flies biting at my neck, my Royal Humpy caught on the rocks and willows behind me. I remember not catching fish and wondering again why I was out there in the stream up to my thighs in water.

I remember, too, that there was then, and has been every time I have gone fishing with my father, a laughing in the water and the pleasant crunch of gravel under my boots and relief offered by the cool wafts of watery air that came up from the stream. There was the rich smell of fish and weeds and pebbles and muck from the undercut banks hung over with grass.

I remember, too, amid the peace and the real joy, a feeling of being trapped. I don't love this, I wanted to shout out so that my

voice echoed off the mountains. I'll never love it like you do. Can't
you see? I'm doing it for you, to be with you. I'm trying. And it
isn't working.

My father agrees to take me to the train station at five in the
morning, long before my train is supposed to leave. Already he has
been up for hours, typing on his computer at the breakfast table.
He will go straight from the train station to his lab and work. He
asks me if I will come and visit him at his cabin in Montana this
summer. I tell him no. I can't spend time with him alone now, until
something, anything, even something small, changes between us.
He asks me what I would like for my graduation present and
suggests some stocks that his parents gave him when he graduated
with his Ph.D. in biology. In the secret, angry language that passes
between us, I hear him saying that he loves me. I want him to say
it out loud. I want him, out loud, to ask me something real about
my life and to tell me something real about his.

Our strongest connection lies in fly fishing, but I want more than
this–I want him to understand me in my wholeness. I want him to
know what else there is about me besides Fishergirl. "You want me
to fish with you," I want to say, "I want you to see who I am."
And I want to tell him this, that I am an ordinary woman who is
thirty-four-years old and owns a stained, smelly fishing vest, only
half of the pockets with anything in them at all. I am an ordinary
woman with a crumpled and eclectic collection of flies, an unused
fly-tying kit, two fly rods, two reels, some cracked nylon wading
shoes, a pair of old-fashioned rubber waders and a couple of books
on fly tying. And besides all of this, I have two cats. I like to drink
strong coffee in the morning. I dance the two-step to country
music. I own a leather miniskirt and purple cowboy boots. I love
my crewcut hair. I sip chamomile tea every night before bed. I
have gone canoeing in the wilderness alone. I won a medal in a
cross-country ski race. I have ordinary desires, to love and be loved

in return. Bills to pay. I am moving to Alaska. And I am a lesbian. He has no idea of who I am.

He hugs me awkwardly, and when I look at him tears are pooling in his eyes. After he leaves I sit in the waiting area and open *The River Why* again. In the last chapters, Gus goes off to a cabin in the woods to fish and be alone, released finally from the pressing of both of his strong-willed parents–the fly fisher and the bait angler–Gus finds himself, and he finds his true love, a glimmering fishing girl with apple blossoms in her hair. In many ways he gives up on his family, gives up about them ever being different, and sets off to have a new life.

One day, upon returning to his cabin, Gus sees, by the stream that runs in front of his house, an old man with a straw hat tipped over one eye, lounging in a chair and fishing with worms. He doesn't recognize the fellow and lets him be. Farther along the stream Gus sees an old woman elegantly decked out in tweeds, fly casting, perfectly. He doesn't recognize her either, but watches her for a while, impressed. Soon he begins to realize that he does know these two. He realizes that they are his mother and father and that they have changed.

When the train arrives I shut my book and move out into the darkness of the platform. I shove my bags aboard and settle into my seat, my face pressed against the window. The train doesn't move for a long time, and I drift off to sleep, dreaming. In the dream my mother is in her kitchen. She wants me to spend more time with my father. "He has something important to show you," she says. My father enters the kitchen, pale and thin, with red and tired eyes, but he is excited, like a boy, showing me his latest miraculous inventions–a new way to fasten rain gutters to the cabin roof, or this, a clip for attaching a cable to a battery, or this, blueprints for a straw toolshed. As I turn away from him, he collapses, folding to the floor like a dropped cloth, and I run to him calling, "Daddy, Daddy, Daddy."

I am startled awake by the train lurching away from the platform with a deep metallic creak and a moan. My heart is pumping unevenly in my chest. I whisper to myself, the words coming out softly and making misty spots on the window glass near my face, "Is it time?" Is it all right to go ahead and admit that I am blood of his blood, that I am my father's daughter, that *this*, that loving to fish, is a gift, that we love some of the same things? In a moment so bright and quick that I hardly know what it is, I understand one thing—no one can really do that to anyone else; no one can really fix or freeze anyone else. But it has been hard to contradict the molding. The more I know who I am, the more I will be able to see who I am, I think, smiling to myself over how much of a riddle it sounds. I am, at least partly, and all on my own, Fishergirl.

As we begin to move, to gather speed, something begins to gather in me—it comes slowly, then faster, then comes on all at once, like a river of heat rolling up from my toes, filling the hollowness of my body, making my scalp prickle, my fingers tremble. This is joy, this thing I was so unaccustomed to not so long ago. *I have changed.* I close my eyes and see a glimmering girl emerge from a silver trout, lithe and shining, running, calling me by my name.

By-Pass

Carol Potter

to my father

How could I have known
when I stood out there in the hall
inking your wrongs against the wall–
how could I have known
how they would want you?

They want you like a field.
Now they are farmers
heading out on their tractors,
your chest is a meadow full of birds–
the tools are sharp in their hands.

I see them digging into you,
parting bone from bone–
they lay you open like a furrow.

I am certain they will find
a cluster of words
huddled in your veins,
a gang of shouting children
flocked in your blood.

They hold you open.
Breath and blood float like a diverted stream
away from you and back again.
Lights stare at your heart;
the doctors hold it in their hands

as if it were a frightened animal
ready to bolt in its own direction.

I tie up my dark horse.
I have made her promise to stand still–
In the hall, my brothers and I wait.
We are carrying buckets of water,
huge sponges and scrub pads.
The water runs down our arms.
The words stare at us steady.

Contributors

Cheryl Burke (aka Cheryl B.) is a writer and seven-year veteran of the New York City spoken-word scene. Her work has appeared in the anthologies *The World in Us* and *Poetry Nation* and in various literary journals. She has performed her work in London and Paris, in Australia and in the Pacific Northwest. She would like to thank Holly Iglesias for her editorial help with this piece.

Karin Cook finished the 1995 New York City Marathon just before dark. Her novel, *What Girls Learn*, won the Booklist/American Library Association Alex Award. She lives in Provincetown, MA and New York City and is currently at work on a new novel

Jewelle Gomez's most recent book is *Don't Explain*. Other work includes *The Gilda Stories*, which won two Lambda Literary Awards; *Oral Tradition: Selected Poems*, and her collection of essays, *Forty-Three Septembers*. She is Executive Director of the Poetry Center and American Poetry Archives at San Francisco State University, where she created the national Audre Lorde Creative Writing Award for state university students.

Janice Gould is the recipient of grants from the National Endowment for the Arts and the Astraea Foundation. She has published two books of poetry, *Beneath My Heart* and *Earthquake Weather*, as well as an artbook/chapbook titled *Alphabet*.

Holly Hughes is an Obie Award-winning performance artist and playwright, with five of her plays included in *Clit Notes: A Sapphic Sample*. She co-edited the anthology of queer solo scripts, *O Solo Homo: The New Queer Performance*.

V. Hunt teaches creative writing at Bainbridge College. Her work has appeared in *BOMB*, *African American Review*, *Apalachee Quarterly*, and in *Every Woman I've Ever Loved: Lesbian Writers on Their Mothers*. She is at work on a memoir titled *Whatever She Wants*.

Gretchen Legler is the author of *All the Powerful Invisible Things: A Sportswoman's Notebook* (Seal, 1995); her essays and short stories have also appeared in *Indiana Review*, *Grain*, *Hurricane Alice*, and numerous anthologies. She teaches creative writing and English at the University of Alaska in Anchorage.

Helena Lipstadt's writing appears in the anthologies *From Memory to Transformation*, *The Challenge of Shalom*, *Every Woman I've Ever Loved: Lesbian Writers on Their Mothers*, and in various journals. She is the author of *Leave Me Signs*, a poetry chapbook written in the northern Negev Desert of Israel, and she is fiction editor of *In the Family*.

Zelda Lockhart is a private consultant for diversity and empowerment workshops in upstate New York. Her fiction, poetry and essays have appeared in *Sojourner*, *Calyx*, and *Word Writes*. Her first novel is forthcoming from Pocket Books.

Bia Lowe's work has appeared in *Harper's*, *Kenyon Review*, *Indivisible: New Short Fiction by West Coast Gay and Lesbian Writers*, *Helter Skelter: L.A. Art in the 1990s*, and *Sister and Brother: Lesbians and Gay Men Write About Their Lives Together*. *Wild Ride: Earthquakes, Sneezes and Other Thrills* is a recent collection of her essays.

Laura Markowitz is publisher and editor of *In the Family: The Magazine for Lesbians, Gays, Bisexuals and Their Relations*, and senior editor of *The Family Therapy Networker*. Winner of a National Magazine Award for writing, her work has appeared in such journals as *Ms.*, *Tricycle*, *Utne Reader*, and others.

Christian McEwen's latest book is *Jo's Girls: Tomboy Tales of High Adventure, True Grit and Real Life* (Beacon Press, 1997). She is also the editor of *Naming the Waves: Contemporary Lesbian Poetry* and *Out the Other Side: Contemporary Lesbian Writing* (Crossing Press, 1989). Her poems, articles and reviews have appeared in *Granta, The American Voice, The Nation,* and *The Voice Literary Supplement.*

Debbra Palmer lives in Portland, Oregon. Her work has appeared in *Calyx, The Portland Review,* and *Mercury.* She enjoys exchanging e-mail with her father because "he writes about the coast, visiting marinas and touring lighthouses."

Carol Potter's most recent collection is *Short History of Pets,* winner of the 1999 Cleveland State University Poetry Center Award. She is also a recipient of the *New Letters* Award for Poetry; her other collections include *Before We Were Born* and *Upside Down in the Dark.*

Minnie Bruce Pratt is a poet and essayist whose most recent book is *Walking Back Up Depot Street.* Other works include the prose collections *S/HE* and *Rebellion: Essays 1980-1991,* and the poetry collections *We Say We Love Each Other* and *Crime Against Nature,* winner of the Lamont Poetry Award.

Peggy Shaw, actor, playwright and producer, has received Obie Awards for *Dress Suits to Hire,* a collaboration with Holly Hughes, and *Belle Reprieve,* a collaboration with the London-based Bloolips. Other work includes *Lust and Comfort, Upwardly Mobile Home, Lesbians Who Kill* and the Jane Chambers Award-winning play *Split Britches.* Her most recent solo work is *Menopausal Gentleman.*

Linda Smukler's collections of poetry include *Normal Sex* and *Home in Three Days, Don't Wash,* with its accompanying CD-ROM. She has received fellowships from the Astraea Foundation and the New York Foundation for the Arts, and is co-author, with Susan Fox Rogers, of *Portraits of Love*.

Tristan Taormino is author of *The Ultimate Guide to Anal Sex for Women* (Cleis Press) and star and director of the video of the same name (Evil Angel Video). She is editor of *On Our Backs*; columnist for *The Village Voice*; sex advice columnist for *Taboo* magazine; producer of www.puckerup.com; and series editor of *Best Lesbian Erotica* (Cleis Press). She also teaches sex workshops and lectures on sex nationwide.

Sheila Ortiz Taylor is a professor of English at Florida State University. Her first novel, the well-loved *Faultline*, is considered the first Chicana lesbian novel. Other works include the novels *Coachella* (UNMP, 1998), *Spring Forward/Fall Back* (Naiad, 1985), and *Southbound* (Naiad, 1990); the poetry collection *Slow Dancing at Miss Polly's*; the memoir *Imaginary Parents*; and the recently completed Arden Benbow novel, *Extranjera*.

Lu Vickers has twice been a recipient of the Florida Arts Council Award, most recently for excerpts from her novel *Snap*. Her short stories, poems and essays have appeared in various journals, including *Salon*, *Hurricane Alice*, *Common Lives*, *Apalachee Quarterly*, and *The Journal of Florida Literature*. She has three sons and teaches fulltime at Tallahassee Community College.

Acknowledgments

"Blood" from *Wild Ride: Earthquakes, Sneezes and Other Thrills*. HarperCollins, New York. ©1995 by Bia Lowe.

Excerpt from "Clit Notes" from *Clit Notes: A Sapphic Sampler*. Grove Press, New York. ©1996 by Holly Hughes.

"A Dad Called Mama" first appeared on the online journal *Salon*, http://www.salon.com. ©1999 by Lu Vickers.

"Duke" from *Forty-Three Septembers*. Firebrand Books, Ithaca, New York. ©1993 by Jewelle Gomez.

"Earbobs" and "Pa" from *S/HE*. Firebrand Books, Ithaca, New York. ©1995 by Minnie Bruce Pratt.

"Fishergirl" from *All the Powerful Invisible Things*. Seal Press, Seattle, Washington. ©1995 by Gretchen Legler.

"Monkey Boy" and "Tales of a Lost Boyhood: Dolls" from *Normal Sex*. Firebrand Books, Ithaca, New York. ©1994 by Linda Smukler.

"Mulberry Tree" from *Present Tense: Writing and Art by Young Women*, Calyx Press, Corvallis, Oregon. ©1996 by Zelda Lockhart.

"My Father" from *Earthquake Weather*. The University of Arizona Press, Tucson. ©1996 by Janice Gould.

"The Trouble with Horses," "The Trouble with Boats," "Because There Was Nothing to Do with the Hands," "By-Pass," from *Before We Were Born*. Alice James Books, Cambridge, Massachusetts. ©1990 by Carol Potter.

"Victoria Told Me Her Secret," from *Present Tense: Writing and Art by Young Women*, Calyx Press, Corvallis, Oregon. ©1996 by Debbra Palmer.

About the Editors

Catherine Reid, PhD, co-editor of *Every Woman I've Ever Loved: Lesbian Writers on Their Mothers*, is an award-winning essayist and fiction writer whose work has appeared in many journals and anthologies. She teaches at Greenfield Community College in Massachusetts and recently completed a memoir, *An Allegory of Want*.

Holly K. Iglesias, PhD, co-editor of *Every Woman I've Ever Loved: Lesbian Writers on Their Mothers*, is the author of three poetry collections: *All That Echoes Her Large* (Permafrost, 1999), *Good Long Enough* (Thorngate Road, 2000), and *Hands-On Saints* (Quale Press, forthcoming). She teaches at the Greenfield Center School and recently received an individual artist grant for poetry from the Massachusetts Cultural Council.